To Helene with Best wishes, cug Rozalise

Under the Vine and the Fig Tree:
The Jews of the Napa Valley

By Lin Weber
for the Jewish Historical
Society of the Napa Valley

Wine Ventures Publishing
PO Box 47
St. Helena, CA 94574

Library of Congress
Control Number 2003107881

History/Jewish Studies

ISBN 0-9667014-4-5

Cover artwork by Dona Kopol Bonick and John Bonick
Cover graphics by Nancy Shapiro

Also by Lin Weber:
Old Napa Valley: The History to 1900
Roots of the Present: Napa Valley 1900-1950

Thanks...

Under the Vine and the Fig Tree: The Jews of the Napa Valley is the brainchild of two visionary women, Donna Mendelsohn and Zoe Kahn, who had a strong feeling that the Napa Valley had an untold Jewish history. As the following pages will demonstrate, they were absolutely correct. Virtually all of the communities in the Napa Valley began with significant contributions from Jewish merchants whose shops made village life possible. Jewish vintners held forth up-valley. As the economy changed, most of these pioneers moved on, but several stayed and became highly respected members of the cities they had helped to found.

Multi-talented Sonya Milton has been my indispensable assistant in researching for this book, having spent hours interviewing many of the contemporary people whose stories it tells.

Graphic artist Nancy Shapiro, noted local photographer Dona Kopol Bonick and artist John Bonick have combined their considerable talents to create the cover, and the gifted Leza Lowitz has served as editor. I'm grateful to them all.

Under the Vine and the Fig Tree is the first publication of the newly formed Jewish Historical Society of the Napa Valley, and I would like to thank its benefactors and advisory board: George Altamura, Moira and Dr. Alvin Lee Block, Dona Kopol Bonick, Elaine and David Freed, Jehon Grist, PhD, Zoe and Howard Kahn, Dorothy Lind, Elizabeth and Jerry Mautner, Donna and David Mendelsohn, Bob and Berit Muh, Louise Packard, Harvey Posert, Ada and Stan Press, Fred Rosenbaum, Julian Weidler and Ernie Weir. The Jewish Community of the Napa Valley, a non-profit organization, provided seed money for the book, and the Peter A. and Vernice H. Gasser Foundation (Joe Peatman, President) also helped underwrite it.

Aaron Kornblum of the Western Jewish History Center at the

Judah L. Magnes Museum in Berkeley was very helpful in allowing me access to the wealth of information housed there, and Jo Morohashi of the Napa Valley Museum in Yountville uncovered some of the rare photos. Thanks, too, to Jack J. Roth of Legendary Graphics for the use of the map of the United States in Yiddish and to Andrea Miller at the De La Salle Institute for her help with information regarding Alfred Fromm. I'm also grateful to Joe Eskanazi of the *Jewish Bulletin of Northern California*, to Steve and Sally Gordon, Jack Paulus, Yvonne Baginsky, the Robert Marshall family, Rabbi David White, Dr. Richard Levy and Tony Petrotta; to my intrepid first-draft reader Nancy Haynes, to Mark Richmond and the Vintage Bank, Cynthia Crawford at Napa Book Tree, as well as to the helpful staff at the Napa and St. Helena Public Libraries.

Above all, I thank my beloved husband Chris for holding down the fort while I explored this fascinating new terrain.

One of the most difficult aspects of researching this book has been determining who among the Napa Valley pioneers was indeed Jewish; a great many of the Valley's earliest residents had German last names that could be either Jew or gentile. There is no Jewish cemetery in Napa County, and a tour of these final resting places revealed very little indication on most headstones as to the departed's ethnicity or religious background. Among the tools I used to assess potential inclusion were such factors as wives' and mothers' maiden names, apparent business associates, trade, place of birth, and newspaper accounts of funeral services. I apologize for any misattributions or omissions.

Lin Weber
St. Helena, CA

(Part One)

Chapter One

Nation will not take up sword against nation
nor will they train for war anymore.
Every man will sit under his own vine
and under his own fig tree,
and no one will make them afraid.
                —*Micah 4:3-4*

FORTY MILES LONG AND NESTLED BETWEEN TWO RANGES OF ANCIENT, low-lying volcanic hills, the Napa Valley is green as emerald in the winter and spring. The hillsides turn gold in the summer, and in the early fall the leaves of the grapevines take on a ruby glow. The heart of America's premium wine industry, it has often been called a kind of Eden.

The Bible makes frequent reference to wine, vines, grapes, vine-yards, even wine presses; and no Eden would be complete without fig trees. To have one's own vine and fig tree would have been, in the symbolism of times long past, to have enjoyed a full measure of personal peace and prosperity. It is imagery that resonates in the hearts of both Jews and Christians even today.

In a very significant way, Jews helped to found the cities of this "Gan Eden," mainly as merchants but also as civic and social leaders. Their numbers and influence began to decline around the turn of the 20th century, and by the mid-1920s there were hardly any Jewish families at all here. It wasn't until the late 1950s that Jewish families began setting down roots again in the wine country.

Who were the pioneer Jews of the Napa Valley? Why did they come? Why did they leave? And what has been the experience of the new generation of Jews in this modern-day paradise? The story of the Jews of the Napa Valley can best be told from the beginning, and the beginning began a long time ago

Soil—territory—has been an important element in Judaism ever since God promised Abraham that a new land awaited the great people he would father. Four hundred years of slavery in Egypt would intervene, but eventually the Jews would claim that land and hold onto at least some of it for 3,700 years: up to the present. They farmed and founded trading centers and established the great city of Jerusalem.

Jews began populating Europe during the height of the Roman Empire. Most got there against their will, dragged to Rome as slaves captured during the Judeo-Roman war, the Jews' 150-year-long effort to throw off imperial rule. They married, had children and eventually were freed. They remained in the imperial city, and though some rose above the poverty level, most did not, enduring difficult lives near the bottom of a social hierarchy that had little sympathy for conquered foes. They built synagogues and kept the faith.[1]

The Romans destroyed the Jews' great Second Temple in 70 CE. It was a sorrow that pierced to the quick. While many Jews remained in Palestine after this critical loss, great numbers dispersed throughout the world. They followed in the wake of the Roman Army and sold wares at the encampments and ancient barbarian villages that would eventually become the major cities of

Europe.

Jewish peddlers were active in Paris and Lyon as early as the year 200 of the Common Era. By 400 CE, Jewish families had settled in Gaul and along the Rhine River. They interacted freely, for the most part, with the Christians, Arians, Zoroastrians, pagans and others who formed the proto-communities of Western Europe.[2]

At first, many of the original European Jews took up farming. Some planted grapes and made wine, as they had in Biblical times, but the ability to engage in this traditional Jewish enterprise would prove to be short-lived.

Agriculture in the Dark Ages depended on the use of slaves and indentured labor, and it was upon this issue that anti-Semitism may first have begun to appear in Europe. According to law, slaves could take on the religion of their masters. When the Jews freed their workers, they increased the numbers of Jewish freemen. This was not acceptable to the Christian leadership, who wanted to augment their numbers through the conversion of non-believers. Prejudicial regulations were thus enacted in many places forbidding Jews to own slaves. With fewer laborers to work their farms and vineyards, more Jews turned to trading.[3]

In order to sell products, these early merchants required the same things modern sales people need: marketable merchandise and customers. To acquire the goods, they connected with friends and co-religionists in other towns who either created goods themselves or traded with manufacturing and bartering contacts even farther afield. To sell what they acquired, they traveled to crossroads throughout Europe and set up stalls that attracted barbarians curious about the wonders of the world beyond their tiny hamlets. They traded. They sold. They brought culture to the exotic and exotica to the cultured, and all benefited.[4]

The Jews thus came to deal with goods that were portable: jewelry, cash, spices, clothing, furs, silks, paper products, wine, liquor, music, medicinal potions.[5]

Geographically fragmented and dependent on a code of laws

already a thousand years old, Jewry held itself together by utilizing a technology that was unknown to most Europeans: the written word. Literacy was a privilege claimed by the Christian clergy, which by 600 CE was an organized and politicized power block. Judaism had no such hierarchy. Its people scattered, it relied on lay leaders within the community who could read and write and lead services. A class of rabbis, experts in the study and application of Jewish religious and civil law, came into being to assist the little enclaves that were forming in some of the larger villages.

The ever-growing mercantile network, combined with the literacy of many Jewish males, gave them an advantage over the Christian majority. In time, many became quite wealthy and could extend credit to their less fortunate gentile townsmen. The lending of credit—banking—was especially lucrative for some and had a positive effect on their communities. Busy marketplaces with interesting things to acquire attracted consumers with coins to spend or valuable items to barter. Populations grew. So did indebtedness.

There was a terrible downside to being both a creditor and an identifiable minority. From time to time, gentiles became resentful of their Jewish merchants and turned on them. The Jews' literacy (a competency among Christians reserved for the clergy) and their ability to prosper without attending church on Sunday contributed to the suspicion that they were somehow in league with the Devil.

The aristocracy took advantage of the Jews' abilities by hiring them as court advisors and financial stewards. It was not uncommon for princes to conscript Jews to serve as tax collectors. When their beleaguered serfs inevitably complained about being parted from their assets, it was not uncommon for the royalty to publicly denounce and even punish the money-gatherers and those who supported them (and keep the cash, of course).[6]

Middle-class guild members excluded Jews from their midst. Passing along their expertise from one generation to the next, families protected their inherited monopolies by assuring the passage of laws that restricted Jews and other outsiders from practicing in their trades.

In time, nearly every European country enacted oppressive laws against their Jewish populations. England expelled its Jews in the 13th century, followed by Italy and, for a time, Portugal. France, Germany, and several other countries forced them to live segregated from the rest of the community and applied restrictions regarding the professions they could undertake.

Periodically, they also killed them, by the hundreds.

The city of Frankfurt, Germany, was representative.[7] By the 12th century, this major central European crossroads was home to a small, thriving community of Jewish merchants and craftsmen. In 1241, however, the townspeople took it upon themselves to attack the city's Jews and killed nearly three-quarters of them. The survivors managed to start over, and within thirty years they were up and running again, but persecutions persisted throughout the century. In the 14th century the government imposed heavy taxes on them, and in the 15th they crammed them together into a walled enclosure called *Judengasse* (Jews' Alley). Isolating the population restricted the gene pool from which Jews were able to reproduce. Two consequences of this were the accelerated transmission of hereditary diseases and the accentuation of selected characteristics. Despite these multiple inhumanities, Jewry not only persevered but produced some of the world's most notable families. Oppenheim, Guggenheim, Haas, Sichel, Schwab and Ochs are some of the names that eventually emerged from the ghetto at Frankfurt.

The most successful of the *Judengasse* families was that of Mayer Amschel Rothschild, a coin dealer with five sons. Nathan, James, Salomon, Amschel and Carl Rothschild set up banking and transportation dynasties in London, Paris, Vienna, Frankfurt, and Naples, respectively. They were bankers to Europe's royalty and made sophisticated, grand scale investments on their own. The degree of wealth that the Rothschild family was able to accumulate still stuns the imagination. Two branches of the Rothschild family—the English and French—eventually became leaders in the wine industry, and one of them would, in the far distant future, have a direct connection with the Napa Valley.[8]

The Rothschild family was an exception in the ease in which its members could travel within the Christian mainstream. So separate were most European Jews from the gentile majority that the Ashkenazi (German) Jews were able, over time, to develop a language of their own called Yiddish, which combined elements of Biblical Hebrew, the tongue of their ancient homeland, with Medieval German and with traces of language from each country through which they had wandered for more than a millennium. Yiddish knit the Jews closer together just as they were being wedged apart from the rest of their countrymen.[9]

Throughout it all the Ashkenazim maintained their literacy and their religion, the one feeding and enhancing the other, and the two together setting them farther and farther apart from the general population.

One country that did not persecute the Jews, at least initially, was Poland. In 1264, King Boleslav actually invited Jewish immigrants to come to his land. He issued an edict promising protection from Christian harassment. Poland's borders expanded in 1569 when it united with Lithuania, further increasing the Jews' opportunities, among which were the rights to distill grain and sell liquor, and to operate inns.[10, 11]

Why the hospitality? Poland was an underdeveloped country compared to its neighbors. Boleslav and his successors wanted what the others had: wise men and money-gatherers. Jewish men were, in effect, the "high tech" secret of medieval power politics. They were literate; their network extended beyond regional boundaries; they were not subject to laws regarding usury and thus could lend money at high rates, and they were not required to attend confession or express allegiance to the clergy. These were enormous advantages over the Christian majority, who usually lacked the rudiments of education, feared the clergy and had little contact with the world at large.

Boleslav's strategy was successful. Poland flourished, and the Jews, delighted to find a place where they could live in peace, prospered. Great numbers immigrated to Poland and settled as farmers, artisans and businessmen.

In 1648, however, Christian peasants in Poland and the Ukraine revolted against the landed class, and since the Jews had become associated with the aristocracy and were identified as creditors and tax collectors, they were targeted for violence. Waves of pogroms swept away thousands. Three hundred Jewish communities were obliterated.

Those who could, ran for their lives. Many went east, into Russia. Russia itself went west, conquering the internally weakened Polish territory and dividing it with the Hapsburgs.

Conquered, too, was Polish Jewry. Over the years the Romanov czars managed to scoop up the Jews and shunt them off to a specially designated area carved out from several provinces, which they called the "Pale of Settlement." In urban ghettos and small settlements called *shtetls*, the Jews of Russia experienced the same religious, cultural, linguistic and genetic concentration they had known elsewhere.

The same anti-Semitism also prevailed, especially among the peasantry. Slavic folk-tales of elegant, blood-sucking vampires needing to be "impaled" drew on fear and hatred of the Jews. So did incredible stories of Jews killing Christian babies and mixing their blood in matzoh; Jews poisoning the wells, and Jews sticking pins in stolen communion wafers to "torture the body of Christ." Anti-Semitic rumors and myths resulted all too often in bloodshed, not only in Russia but throughout Europe.

Anti-Semitism had become an integral part of Old World culture, embedded, so it seemed, in its DNA. Hope for the Jews would require a cosmic act: nothing less than the appearance of a New World.

Luckily, such a world happened to show up. The very first European documented to have set foot on it was Luis de Torres, Christopher Columbus' interpreter, who had been baptized just before leaving Spain. The expediency of his christening did not alter his ancestry: de Torres was a Sephardic (Spanish) Jew. Among the dozen or so languages de Torres spoke was Hebrew. Columbus believed they were sailing the back way to the Far East, and he expected to find there one or more of the lost tribes of Israel. He may have been disappointed when the natives he met couldn't understand a word de Torres said.[13]

There were five Sephardim altogether on Columbus' voyage, among them Columbus' personal physician and his navigator. Some even speculate that Columbus himself might have been at least partly Jewish. The fact that the Niña, Pinta and Santa Maria left the day after Ferdinand and Isabella issued an edict expelling the Jews and the Muslims from Spain is cited as one piece of evidence.

The polyglot de Torres was not unique in his mastery of several languages. Many Spanish Jews were very well educated, and there were very many Spanish Jews. Jews had trickled into Spain for several centuries and met with repressive treatment by the ruling Visigoths. The Visigoths fell from power when Muslim armies swept across North Africa in the late 600s and crossed the Strait of Gibraltar. In 711 the Muslims took control of Iberia all the way to the Pyrenees. They brought with them abilities in linguistics, medicine and mathematics that astounded the mostly illiterate Visigoth establishment.[14]

More Jews from Babylon, Judea and other Middle Eastern places followed the conquering Muslims into Spain. They settled, did well, and enjoyed a Golden Age of peace and prosperity that lasted for seven centuries. Some of the Sephardim served in the highest levels of the Spanish court, married non-Jews and enjoyed significant wealth. They farmed, practiced medicine and engaged in the entire spectrum of business and artistic enterprise.

And then it ended. By 1492 the Visigoths' Christian descendents had managed to hound and harass their Semitic population out of influence and into submission. On August 2 of that year, between 150,000 and 200,000 people were turned out of their homes in the ghettos to which they had been confined. The Jews who managed to stay in Spain were forced to convert to Christianity or lie about their heritage. A great number fled to France, especially to the Provence region.[15]

De Torres and Columbus' other Jewish crewmen were the first wave in a tide of Sephardim who took to the sea to avoid persecution. Sephardic Jews served in Hernando Cortes' army and in the retinue of other explorers who hacked their way through the jungle. As soldiers and later as colonists, they helped to populate Mexico and Central America with Spanish speakers.

Were the truth of their ancestry to be revealed, however, they would have been executed. The infamous Spanish Inquisition soon spanned the Atlantic. Hundreds of Jews were discovered and burned at the stake.

Portuguese Jews were among the first to book passage to the vast and unexplored tropic of Brazil, recently claimed for their country by the naval commander Pedro Cabral. The most successful colony was on the island of Recife, where a relatively large group of Sephardim enjoyed balmy weather and financial reward as exporters of rarities like sugarcane, tobacco, and tropical foods. They practiced their Judaism secretly, for the torches of the Inquisition were always close at hand.

Holland invaded and conquered Brazil. The Dutch did not participate in the Inquisition and, in fact, were among the more tolerant European countries. Immediately, the Recife Jews cast off their cloaks of secrecy and worshiped openly. They continued to prosper until Portugal staged a counter-attack in 1654 and drove out the Dutch.

Having tipped their hand, the Jews now had to flee. A boatload of them arrived in the Dutch colony of New Amsterdam (later New York). Governor Peter Stuyvesant received them with the greatest reluctance. Had the Dutch West Indian Company not intervened, he would probably have ordered them to leave.[16]

Despite the chilly welcome of the Recife boatload, small numbers of Jewish immigrants trickled into the American colonies. Shearith Israel, the first permanent synagogue in America, was established in Manhattan in 1731, and by 1815 it had a lively congregation of 855 members, a *cheder* (school), and a *mikveh* (ritual bath). Similar synagogues formed in Philadelphia, Boston, Charleston and Newport.

By the time of the Revolutionary War, there were some 2,000 American Jews, many of them living in New York State, Pennsylvania and in the American south, most of them Sephardic. They fought with valor for their fledgling country. Francis Salvador, for example, was the first patriot killed in Georgia. Financier Haym Salomon endured a different form of martyrdom. He advanced his entire fortune, $200,000, to the cause of freedom, and was never reimbursed.

In gratitude for the contributions of these and other Jews during the war, George Washington lent his blessing in 1790 to the Jews of Rhode Island. He wrote:

> May the children of the stock of Abraham
> who dwell in the land continue to merit
> and enjoy the goodwill of the other inhab-
> itants. While everyone shall sit safely under
> his own vine and fig-tree and there shall
> be none to make him afraid.[17]

The reference to safety among the figs and grapes is a quotation from the prophet Micah, where he speaks of the new Zion. In this new Promised Land, the Lord Himself will settle disputes, and nations will "beat their swords into plowshares and spears into pruning hooks." The quest for Zion would occupy the thoughts of many Jews in years to come.

Largely Protestant, Americans were on the whole more literate than Europeans and had a far better grasp of the Bible than the populace in Catholic countries, where the scriptures were still written in Latin. In a land where everyone was a relative newcomer, there were few aristocrats to double-cross their bankers and tax collectors. Here, the Jews faced an entirely different problem: assimilation, that is, the loss of their Judaism by becoming absorbed into the dominant culture. Free from the ghetto, free to marry, free to engage in any trade they chose, many American Sephardim abandoned their Jewish identity in order to participate fully with their friendly fellow colonists

Xenophobia, fear of the different, has always been a strong element in human nature, even in places like America, which theoretically valued diversity. Jews who maintained their Jewishness in face of the very strong assimilative forces at work in the young republic often lived lonely, isolated lives on the margins of their communities. Many worked as peddlers, trading or selling their wares with householders in the outlying rural areas, just as their forebears had done in the Old World for hundreds of years. Under threat of thieves, accidents, sickness and the weather, these hardy small businessmen roamed the countryside (and sometimes the city streets) on foot. Others had a horse or two, and, if they were moderately well off, a wagon. Besides dry goods like textiles, notions and ready-to-wear clothing, their packs or carts could include such diverse merchandise as groceries, paper products, hardware, patent medicines, cigars and furniture. Some carried jewelry, watches and clocks.[18]

The most fortunate would eventually return to urban areas, establish stores and enjoy prestige in the city by dint of the merchandise they provided and the generous donations they made to worthy causes. They hired others to peddle their wares, often keeping them on salary or giving them a percentage of the profit. They participated in the network of manufacturers and suppliers of certain goods that had been part and parcel of the Jewish experience since the days of the Roman emperors.

But by 1800 relatively few had yet been able to enjoy this level of success while maintaining their Judaism. They had plenty of stamina; all they needed was a lucky break.

Meanwhile, across the ocean, the Enlightenment, the French Revolution and Napoleon's reforms had triggered a liberal movement among Christians that promoted a degree of religious tolerance such as that demonstrated by the American president. At the same time, many European Jews were examining their Jewishness. Moses Mendelssohn and other Jewish leaders urged their followers to abandon many of the traditional expressions of their faith (to avoid seeming "too Jewish"), so that the group as a whole could make inroads into the life of a world which might finally be more accepting. This became known as the Jewish Reform Movement. (Reform Judaism was destined to play an important role in the development of California, as shall be seen, and would finally impact the Napa Valley.)

The Reform Movement took root in Germany in the context of this homogenizing trend. The friendlier atmosphere lured many Jews to try to blend into gentile society, as their cousins were doing in America. Those who did sometimes lost much of what had distinguished them as Jews. Mendelssohn's grandson Felix, for example, became a highly honored composer and musician and completely abandoned his Judaism. It was a strategy many of his peers would adopt.

Napoleon altered much more than the map of Europe; he effected far-reaching internal changes on several levels. He weakened the long-held power of the privileged; he also cut into certain bastions of the middle class. One of his targets was the guild system. Artisan families who had dominated what little industry the continent had known had resisted change and thus discouraged competition, which thwarted technological development. Napoleon sought to correct this and follow the industrial model that England had initiated when it ended its guild system.

The guilds had been especially repressive in Germany. Thanks to Napoleon's reforms, the first half of the 19th century saw the unprecedented growth of a manufacturing middle class in Germany that featured a preponderance of Ashkenazim. Bottled up for some 1800 years, their creative and entrepreneurial energy exploded in a burst of mercantile, financial, and cultural activity.

Well-placed Jews in Germany, Austria and Prussia prospered. Their sons attended prestigious schools and married into other well-placed families, some of them Christian. In keeping with the ancient Jewish tradition of charity, the wealthiest among them gave back generously to their communities, which won them favor and recognition, at least temporarily.

When they learned of the success their contemporaries were enjoying in Germany, struggling Polish Jews began migrating west. Unaffected by the Reform movement, these *Ostjuden* (eastern Jews) often displayed much of what the German Jews were trying to shed. After decades of imprisonment in the Pale, they were poor, pious and provincial: an embarrassment to the erudite Teutons. Tension developed within Judaism between the more traditional *Ostjuden* and the wealthier, cosmopolitan Reform Jews.

But the window of opportunity that had opened in Germany showed signs of closing. In 1848 and 1849 a series of riots in major German cities pitted the old regime, including middle-class gentile artisans, against the philosophical liberals and their supporters. Once again, the Jews were seen as usurping aliens. The German economy plunged. Fearful that the old anti-Semitic repressions might return, Jews who could afford it, mainly Reform Jews, began to leave Germany.[19]

Great numbers of them sailed to America. They came just in time to take part in a momentous event...

Chapter Two

I lift up my eyes to the hills—
Where does my help come from?
—Psalm 121

THE YEAR 1848 HELD A MARVEL OF SYNCHRONICITIES. THE VERY
moment that Jewish passengers were disembarking in New York
City, armed American soldiers on the other side of the continent
were coming ashore to engage in battle. The Mexican-American
War of 1846-48 resulted in the United States' annexation of
California.

Americans had been scaling the Sierras in increasing numbers
since 1841. Among the very first of the pioneers to settle in what
would become Napa County was Joseph Chiles, a Christian ex-sol-
dier whose dream was to find a peaceful, fertile spot to build a
home and raise his children. He found the place along a clear,
unspoiled stream in a narrow, wooded valley that would one day
bear his name: Chiles Valley, near the soon-to-be county's geo-
graphical center. Among those who crossed the snowy mountains
with him was Elias Barnett, who settled in Pope Valley, an oak-
studded expanse to the northeast of Chiles.

A group of hunters made a semi-permanent encampment near what has become Calistoga, where hot springs bubbling up from the ground had once attracted a large Native American population. The Indians' numbers had been decimated by disease, subjugation by the Spanish and Mexicans and further torment by the hunters and other ruffians.

An English doctor with a penchant for alcohol owned 17,000 acres in the heart of the Valley. The Mexican government had granted Edward Turner Bale this vast tract of land after he married a niece of the administrator, Mariano Vallejo.

A retired mountain man, George Yount, was the first Caucasian to live in the Napa Valley. He built a wooden, Kentucky-style fortress for protection against the natives, but as they died off or receded into the safety of the northern hills, he would prepare himself a more comfortable dwelling.

A few Mexican *vaqueros* ran horses in the southern part of the Valley for wealthy Mexican grant holders. They had adobes in a small pueblo at the head of the tidewater of the gentle river that wound through the tule rushes.

It was here that a handful of American pioneers plotted out a town in that auspicious year, 1848. Once the shoulder-high wild grasses were mowed and the bears were chased away, it would be an ideal place for shipping and commerce, they believed. Its mild climate would beckon hundreds, perhaps thousands of homesteaders from the States, and the first to own land there and set up shop would get rich from the hordes who would eventually follow. Nathan Coombs, who owned the river-fronting parcel, thought his new town would be called "Coombsville." Instead folks called it "Napa City."

While workers were hammering the roof on Napa City's first building (a saloon), an American laboring to build a mill in the Sierra foothills noticed a yellow sparkle in the water. He pulled out a pea-sized rock and showed it to his boss, James Marshall. It was gold. They tried to keep the find a secret, but word got out, thanks mainly to Sam Brannan, the editor-publisher of San Francisco's first newspaper.

Brannan bought land in the foothills and arranged for a large shipment of mining supplies. When everything was ready, he publicized the discovery of gold in his newspaper, sent copies all over the country and to China and waited for the world to rush in.

In it rushed. Leading the parade were thousands of strapping young ex-soldiers who were mustered out from the Mexican-American War with no means back home and, suddenly, no good reason to leave. Armed with the shovels and pans they had purchased from Brannan, they headed for the Sierra foothills and tried to pluck their fortunes from the streams. Many of these '48rs found gold. They scooped up treasure by the sackful and returned home rich, able to build large houses for themselves and live as comfortably as was possible in the California interior. Some of them came to the Napa Valley.

Except for the extremely lucky, however, the real money was not to be made in panning for gold but in following Brannan's lead. Far from commercial centers, the miners would be a splendid market for the necessities of life. This fact was not lost on a generation of Jewish men, including those who had just left Germany to get away from the repressions of 1848.

Gathering all the cash they could find and as much merchandise as they could manage, fresh immigrants and former peddlers booked passage on steamers and braved the difficult passage across the Isthmus of Panama to the Pacific Ocean or the longer but no less risky passage around Cape Horn at the tip of South America. Some died along the way, but between 1849 and 1860, hundreds of Jewish entrepreneurs came to San Francisco and the gold country, not necessarily to mine, but mainly to sell.

One such man was Freedman Levinson, a Prussian who left home with his young wife, Dora Shemanski Levinson, when he was twenty-seven and she twenty-one. They stayed for about a year with relatives (hers, perhaps) in New York and got a sense of the lay of the land. Then they gathered all the money they could and perhaps some merchandise and headed west, crossing Central America via the mosquito-infested Isthmus.[20]

They were drawn to the tiny town of Napa, a muddy, dusty hangout for miners down from the digs with gold dust to spend. The place must have been quite a shock to the cultured Dora.

> Each man was a 'law unto himself.' Very
> few had settled habitations. Rents even for
> the meanest structures were enormous.
> The mass of the people had no family
> ties to hold them in check, and there
> were no places of public resort excepting
> barrooms, saloons and gambling houses. [21]

As the historian C.A. Menefee points out, the cost of doing business in Napa City in an actual building was very high. This was because actual buildings were, in the beginning, few. Most of Napa City's first merchants held forth from wagons and tents and from boats moored in the Napa River. When their merchandise ran out, they closed up shop and went back to their supplier (usually a relative or employer in San Francisco) for more.

Freedman Levinson set up a small general store on Main Street that eventually carried toys as well as daily necessities, although there were few children in the area in the town's infancy. There were no schools, no places of worship, no parks, no services of any kind to address the needs of a younger generation.

Business was usually conducted in gold dust. Levinson and Napa's other original merchants had scales on their counters for weighing the value of the offerings in the customers' little bags. They became skilled in identifying real gold from fake.

Many little businesses vied for the miners' dust. Freedman Levinson had plenty of competition, and more than a few of his competitors were fellow Jews. Like other recent immigrants,

Levinson was handicapped by a limited English vocabulary and a heavy accent, so to attract shoppers he kept a pet canary in a cage outside his store's front door.

Zubrick & Keifer were among the first grocers in the new town.[22] M. Haller was proprietor of a furniture store that was located across from the little Courthouse. Julius Salomonson sold dry goods and clothing not far away, but he left the shop to enter the lumber business with John Gillam (not a Jew), who bought and leased timberland all over the valley.[23]   Photographs of the 1870s and '80s indicate that many of the Valley's slopes were far more thinly vegetated than today, the work, in part, of Salomonson and Gillam.

Levinson, Haller and Salomonson were able to do in Napa something that they would not have been able to do in Europe: They joined a gentile men's fraternity. All three were "Brothers of the Fifth Degree" in the Independent Order of Odd Fellows, Napa Lodge No. 18, established in 1853.

Joining them in town was another Jewish family, the Haas brothers. Martin, Solomon and David Haas, young Germans, had already established themselves as "importers and jobbers in blankbooks, stationery and wrapping paper" at Number 227 Front Street in San Francisco, an area heavily populated by Jewish businesses. They also had a store in Vallejo, another newly forming city to the south in Solano County.

The Haases opened their Napa branch at 40 Main Street with Martin as the first proprietor. They sold books, stationery, fancy goods, perfumes, cigars, tobacco, and Rosenbaum's bitters, a patent medicine. Another section of the store was devoted to the sales of the Florence Sewing machine.

Other Haases had done business in Nevada City at the very start of the Gold Rush. Samuel Haas was known there as "Cheap John." He got into some difficulty there when he appeared to thwart a law banning business on Sundays. After the local newspaper editor took him to task for selling on the Christian Sabbath, Samuel explained that he stayed open because his competitor did. The editor apologized to him in print, something that never would have happened in his native country.[24]

The Napa Haases advertised the source of many of their products. They were connected with a store in New York City at 51 Maiden Lane that was undoubtedly operated by another member of the family who had arrived in America earlier and done well.

As it was in Europe, the presence of Jewish-run businesses was a good sign for a town's economy, because it implied both the presence of interesting merchandise from afar and a market of customers with money to spend. By the start of the Civil War, Napa City was an important center of commerce, its river jammed with freight and its sidewalks crowded with Jewish and gentile enterprises. The *Pacific Echo*, a southern-leaning newspaper published there, carried advertisements in 1862 for quite a few of them, including the Haases. (The fact that they advertised with a Confederate sympathizer did not imply agreement with the Echo's editorial slant; most of them also ran ads in the Yankee paper, the *Napa Daily Register*.)

August Weinlander, a Bavarian Jew, had a "cheap variety store" just down the street from the Haases. Gustave Boukofsky & Company competed with Weinlander. Boukovsky's place was on the corner of Main and First Streets. Besides the ubiquitous fancy and dry goods, the Prussian-born Boukofsky also sold groceries, boots, shoes, hats, crockery, hardware and groceries, and he was open to receiving produce in payment for goods. His newspaper ads spoke of a "New Store and New Goods." He had connections with a San Francisco merchandiser whose contacts back east provided those "new goods."

If Boukofsky's wares didn't suit, Napa shoppers could visit C. Isaacs' clothing store on Main, between First and Second Streets. Isaacs, a Pole, arrived in the United States in 1854, stayed in New York for two years and then traveled to San Francisco with his family in 1856, probably with a shipment of goods. They set up shop in Napa in 1857. His daughter Rebecca married Simon Galewsky, and the young couple opened a branch store up the valley in St. Helena, one of the first enterprises in that fledgling community. The Galewskys would become very important figures there.

Three Juliuses did business in Napa. Besides the aforementioned Julius Salomonson, Julius Goldsmith had a "fancy and dry goods" emporium on First Street between Main and Brown; but it was at Julius Israelsky's "new cash store," where "high prices are put to flight."[25]

Israelsky was among the most successful of the early Napa merchants. Gustave Boukofsky moved into the first Israelsky store when Israelsky took over the failed enterprise of two gentiles, Parks and Pierson, at 38 Main Street. Israelsky was a member of the Odd Fellows and a principal partner in the Silver Bow Mining Company in Pope Valley, along with P.E. Perl and J.H. Kester, who were probably also Jewish.[26]   Three generations of Israelskys would eventually make Napa their home.

If hunger gnawed while shopping, one could stop to nosh a goodie at Max Begelspecker's Star Bakery on First Street. Begelspecker held on to the business for more than thirty years. He finally sold out to M. Cohen in 1890. Cohen once ran a store in the tiny and now extinct town of Monticello in Berryessa Valley.

Jewelry and timepieces, other stock items in the Jewish peddler's pack, could also be bought from Jewish proprietors in Napa. B.F. Winkler was a watchmaker and jeweler with a store "above the Napa Hotel" on Main Street (there were no street addresses in Napa's earliest days).

Yet another Jewish businessman, Solomon Cahen, sold "goods at New York prices" at his shop on First Street between Main and Brown. New York prices were low compared with the cost of goods in Napa City during the mid 19th century.

One of the secrets to mercantile success in the first decades of

California's statehood was to link up with a supplier/manufacturer and establish a flow of goods and payment across the continent. Express companies like Wells, Fargo conveyed the payments (almost always in gold), but the goods still had to come by way of Panama, overland by wagon or around the Horn.

California prices were very high, because merchandising, like gold mining, was a chancey business. Ships sank, stages got robbed, debtors slipped out of town without paying. Most of the proprietors only stayed a few years, although some endured for decades and became fixtures in the community. M. Haller's furniture store on the corner of Second and Brown Streets did well. By 1873 Haller could advertise himself as the "Pioneer Furniture Dealer." Jews would come to play a very important role in California's furniture business in the decades to come, and Haller's was one of the first.

The Haases also prospered. Martin Haas may have moved away, because David took over the store and eventually became a director of the Bank of Napa, which boasted $250,000 in capital in 1872—a fortune in those days. Sol remained in business with David and married a gentile woman, Emma Howland, whose father was the Napa postmaster.

Merchants often became bankers, and David Haas' seat on the board of the Bank of Napa may have been a direct result of extending credit, with interest, to his customers. It was also common for people to leave their gold dust with a trusted merchant for safekeeping. As a tobacconist, David Haas supplied a commodity in much demand (as did D.S. Tallman, probably also Jewish, in his competing stationery store down the street).

But it was the Levinsons, one of the very first Jewish families to come to the Napa Valley, whose contribution was the most profound and long-lasting. Freedman and Dora had six children, three girls and three boys. They created a population explosion. The supply of playthings at the store (and the canary) may have helped to win the Levinson kids a great deal of popularity with their peers.

All of the Levinson children proved to have excellent people skills, assets that allowed them to enjoy a large circle of friends both Jewish and gentile.

Other communities also began to congeal in the Napa Valley, and the presence of Jewish businessmen helped these new villages survive their infancies.

Chapter Three

*The men of Hiram and the men of Solomon
brought gold from Ophir...*
—*2 Chronicles 9:10*

IN 1852, TWO SEASONED PIONEERS HOME FROM THE PLACER MINES stumbled upon some thermal pools in a secluded mid-valley side canyon. The stream that ran through it smelled strongly of sulphur, and minerals coated its stony bed. Knowing they had found a gem, they sold the place to an investment company, who then passed it on to a pair of developers. They named it "White Sulphur Springs" like a similar place in Virginia that was founded at around the same time.

WSS became California's first resort. Newly rich miners, the merchants most successful at supplying them, and the sons and daughters of old, wealthy aristocrats who formed San Francisco's upper crust came to take the waters at this popular gathering place. The latter were mostly southerners and would have appreciated dipping their toes in the western version of the famous Virginian spa.

A little town grew up nearby, attracting not only the tourists from the spa but the pioneer families who had come before, during and after the Gold Rush to start new lives in California. "Hot Springs Township" became identified as a fine place for some to live and for others to enjoy rest and recreation. Sometime during the late 1850s the village took on the name "St. Helena."

Among Hot Springs/St. Helena's earliest residents were several Jewish families. The Level brothers, Sephardic Jews, started a business there before the Civil War.[27] Leon Level was the up-valley agent for the pro-Union Napa newspaper, an arrangement that ended in 1862 when the Levels left town. St. Helena was strongly pro-South at the start of the war; the Levels' affiliation is unknown.

A faded but mostly legible farewell note survives in the *Napa Weekly Reporter,* October 25, 1862:

> To the citizens of St. Helena and vicinity:
> We take this method to wish you all a
> friendly Good Bye and to thank you for
> the liberal patronage extended to us
> during our sojourn of five years in your
> beautiful valley. The remembrance of
> your many kindnesses shall ever live
> in our hearts wherever we may be,
> whether in "Sunny France" or elsewhere.
> Those still indebted to us will find
> their accounts and can settle with our
> successors, Lazarus Brothers, to whom
> we bespeak a part of the patronage so
> liberally extended to us, knowing them to
> be honest and worthy of the same.
>   Level Brothers [28]

The Levels may indeed have returned to "sunny France" after selling the store.

The Lazarus family took over.[29] Leopold Lazarus was also French. He left his homeland in 1848 at the age of twenty-one and sailed to New Orleans.[30] The Lazarus name had prestige. Emma

Lazarus was a contemporary of Longfellow's who wrote of Jewish life in a poem called "In the Jewish Synagogue at Newport." She was the first Jewish woman in America to gain national recognition. Another of Lazarus' poems would grace a symbol of American freedom, the Statue of Liberty, as shall be described later.[31]

Leopold Lazarus was blessed with an adventurous spirit. Excited by news of the discovery in the Sierras, he boarded a steamer to Panama and became part of the Gold Rush. He worked in a clothing store in San Francisco for a year while his English improved, then moved to San Jose, where he sold dry goods until around 1857. He went to Vallejo and ran a restaurant (a French one, no doubt), where his clientele would have consisted of gold miners and travelers on the way to Napa and the resort at Hot Springs.

Before long he, too, wanted to try his hand at wresting gold from the earth. He opened a store in the White Mountain Mining District, Tulare County. When things got quiet he looked for treasure. It was somewhat unusual for Jews to do the actual mining; most of the Jewish men in the gold country supported the miners by selling wares and providing other services. Lazarus, however, was gregarious and may have partnered with a group of gentiles in the mining enterprise.

There was little anti-Semitism among the miners.[32] Church attendance was not a high priority, and a man's beliefs were relatively unimportant. Nor were his origins; indeed, many of the men there were eager to escape their histories and start afresh. The foothills were alive with men from around the world who were there for one thing only: to strike it rich. The most common objection to the Jews was that they didn't work with their hands. Brawn and not brains was the valued virtue for the '49rs.[33]

The groups who did receive the kind of mistreatment the Jews had known in Europe were the Native Americans, whose numbers were dwindling; the Mexicans, who were relatively few, and the

Chinese. The California legislature passed discriminatory laws tax-
ing foreigners, but the only foreigners regularly subjected to it were
the Asians and the Mexicans, the latter not being foreign at all in
most cases. California's first legislators wrote "Whites Only" laws
enjoining Asians from owning property.

Leopold Lazarus did well, perhaps not as a miner but as a merchant, where he was among those who extended credit and enjoyed
a reliable return on investment. In 1862 he came to the Napa Valley
with some money in his pocket and did what most Jewish men did:
started a store. His was in St. Helena, across from the Levels, with
whom he could speak French.

In 1863 he joined forces with another Sephardic family, marrying Julia Straus, a young woman from Alsace who was living in
San Francisco. Given the affection of southern aristocrats for the
French, it is likely that Julia received a friendly greeting in the city
and enjoyed some prestige.

Like Leopold Lazarus, the Strauses had made New Orleans
their first stop in the new world, arriving there in 1853 and staying
for at least six years. Young Joseph Straus, Julia's brother, clerked
at a store there. He may have enlisted in the Confederate Army and
fought in the Civil War. After Appomattox, he traveled to San
Francisco the long way, around the Horn, which suggests that he
came with merchandise and needed cargo space. Any cargo that Joe
Straus had to sell may well have come directly from France, since
Confederate manufacturing was a smoldering ruin in 1865.[34]

Six months later Joe and whatever cargo he may have shep-
herded arrived in San Francisco. He came straight to the Napa
Valley, where he joined his brother-in-law, Leopold Lazarus, in the
St. Helena store. He only stayed a year. For the next three years he
traveled about exploring the countryside, clerking in stores to cover
his expenses.

He returned in 1870 with a wife, Janett Levy, another Sephardi
from France, and resumed work with Lazarus.[35]   E.A. Straus also
worked at the store. Joe and E.A. both joined the St. Helena Odd

Fellows lodge, and Joe was a charter member of the "Ancient Order of United Workmen," another fraternal organization. Perhaps to highlight the Straus' connection with Janett Levy's family, they renamed the store Lazarus & Levy.[36]

Leopold Lazarus became the local agent for Wells, Fargo, which served the town as a post office and an express service and later as a bank. The express and banking work was so consuming that in 1875 Lazarus sold the old Level store to the Strauses. He turned the Lazarus & Levy site into a post office/Wells, Fargo bureau and worked there full time.

Leopold's congeniality, combined with his role as a banker/postmaster, appealed to his fellow St. Helenans, who elected him to serve as city Treasurer. It was a post to which he was reappointed year after year.

Joe Straus also prospered, and his success bred envy. M. Bloch, who had a store in Napa, tried to snatch away some of Straus' customers by renting space near the National Hotel in 1877 and calling his place the "largest clothing store in St. Helena." His prices, he claimed, were "cheaper than the cheapest" and "fully 25 per cent cheaper than any other house."[37] A Napa retailer named Alden also opened a St. Helena branch,[38] and David Haas teamed up with a man named Ford to start a clothing store that also sold sewing machines. St. Helenans were treated to a kind of merchants' war, where Straus, Alden, Bloch and Haas all competed for the young town's dollars.

David Haas was the first to cry Uncle. He gathered his goods and moved to Lakeport. Said the *St. Helena Star*, "We are glad to say they did well here, disposing of an immense amount of goods. We wish them success and a speedy return to St. Helena."[39] The Haas Brothers never did come back to the wine town, however. In 1879 their expenditures outpaced their assets to the point where they were $24,000 in debt to some of the largest wholesale book dealers and tobacconists in San Francisco. Their creditors allowed them to stay in business (Haas paid them 40¢ to the dollar), but their days of expansion were over, at least for a while.[40]

Neither the Levels, Lazarus and Levy nor the Haas brothers were as important to the congealing of St. Helena, however, as was the Galewsky family. Simon and his wife Rebecca Isaacs Galewsky established a general store on Main Street in 1858 that supplied the town's pioneers with their daily necessities. Their first child, Emanuel, was born in 1860, and both father and son contracted tuberculosis. Emanuel struggled on, but Simon succumbed from it in 1868, and Rebecca immediately remarried another Galewsky, perhaps Simon's brother. "D. Galewsky" took over the proprietorship. In 1874 he sold half of the space to W.A.C. Smith, who worked at least part of the time as a schoolteacher. Young Emanuel was one of Smith's star pupils.

Rebecca Galewsky had a daughter, Sarah, born in 1868, and then in 1879, Joe came along. Joe Galewsky could have been a prototype for the Little Rascals. One of his locally famous pranks involved a goat. Joe tied one end of a very long rope to the bell on top of the school and the other end to the goat's collar, so that whenever the animal walked about, the school bell rang. The scene of baffled teacher, oblivious goat and hysterically laughing children lived on in the memory of many for years. He also masterminded the hoisting of a wagon onto the school's rooftop, causing classes to be canceled until it could be gotten down. One day Joe engaged a shopkeeper in a lively conversation while handing him an empty vinegar bottle to fill from the cask in the grocery store. While the shopkeeper and Joe talked (and a group of Joe's friends watched from behind the shelves), the former filled the bottle—which had no bottom, causing the vinegar to pour all over the poor man's shoes.[41] Perhaps not surprisingly, Joe wanted to become a politician.

In 1879 another Jewish merchant happened through St. Helena, this one not a French Sephardi of urbane tastes or a Napa merchant hoping to expand, but a Hungarian peddler. It was he who would finally win the battle of the Jewish merchants.

Abraham Goodman had arrived in the United States in 1876 and made his way to Cincinnati, a city situated on a river and therefore a hub of commerce. Cincinnati had a large Jewish population and a congregation that dated back to 1824. It was a stopping-off place for travelers but especially important for traders who shipped goods from its port on the Ohio River down to New Orleans on the Mississippi. Many of its pioneer settlers spoke German. German-speaking Jewish merchants thus found it a very suitable place to touch down before venturing out into the American countryside. Abraham Goodman was one of many hundreds of Ashkenazim who got their bearings in the New World by staying first in Cincinnati; just as many Sephardim went first to Newport, Rhode Island or New Orleans. (A third river city with a thriving Jewish population in the mid-19th century was Memphis, Tennessee, for the same reasons; it had an excellent port and a large German-speaking population.[42])

Having made contact with a supplier in San Francisco, Abraham Goodman found himself in St. Helena. The story goes that his wagon broke down in the center of town, and the townspeople were so thrilled with the wares he was hauling that they bought him out. This is unlikely, as there were already more than enough stores in Hot Springs/St. Helena that carried the things liable to be found in a peddler's cart. More reasonable is the idea that Goodman found so many Jewish businessmen tending shop in St. Helena—and the prospects for success so rosy—that he felt comfortable settling down there for a while.

An early photograph of the A. Goodman & Co. building, which was on the northwest corner of Main and Spring Streets, showed him to have been in partnership with N. Lauter selling clothing and shoes and "dry and fancy goods." It is unknown how long Goodman and the tall, dapper Nathan Lauter remained in partnership. Lauter's daughter Hilda was born in Napa County and eventually married a man surnamed Haber.[43] Lauter himself, together with the Levy Brothers, later opened a store at Cape Nome in Alaska, hoping to take advantage of the gold rush in the Klondike. Leopold Lazarus' son Sylvain spent time there, as well.[44]

The old photograph also shows a lava mounting block engraved "AG" near the edge of the wooden sidewalk. It was there to help passengers on and off their horses and buggies. Two hitching rails in front of the building kept the animals from straying while their owners shopped. These transportation aids suggest that Goodman and Lauter had an eye for customer-pleasing extras, which probably meant higher prices but better quality merchandise than their cut-rate competitors could offer. With St. Helenans even then, this formula had staying power.

By 1880 St. Helena was thriving. The wine industry was starting to take off, a lively consumer market had developed, and the town was attracting a bevy of merchants, many of them Jewish. Success may have bred envy, but it also bred more success.

Chapter Four

...a hundred talents of silver, a hundred
cors of wheat, a hundred baths of wine,
a hundred baths of olive oil
—Ezra 7:22

SAM BRANNAN'S PROMOTION OF THE GOLDEN DISCOVERY IN THE foothills triggered the stampede he was hoping for. His merchandising methods made him the richest man in California, at least for a while. Having helped himself and hundreds of others prosper from the gold fields that he touted, he set about to create a place for people to spend their new wealth.

Brannan had traveled to Europe and enjoyed the spas there. Impressed with the success of nearby White Sulphur Springs, he decided to create a resort of his own at the head of the Valley, where hot water gurgled up from the ground in abundance. He bought and sued for all the land he could get, and by 1862 he was ready for the grand opening of "the Saratoga of California." Drunk with more than just enthusiasm, however, he raised his glass to toast the place, and called it instead "the Calistoga of Sarafornia." Calistoga it was, from then on.

The centerpiece of the 2,000-acre resort was the Hot Springs Hotel and its associated guest cottages. Sam spent at least half a million dollars on the resort, hoping to lure thousands of tourists. Some who came to enjoy the sunny Calistoga weather were successful Jewish businessmen. An entry in the June 9, 1872 issue of the *Calistoga Tribune* reported that H. Cohen, C. Sutro and Joel Lightner arrived at the hotel as one party. E. Rother and H. Balzer, each with "a lady" also came to the hotel that day.[45] Paid female companionship was a popular option among gentlemen of means, and one of the few occupations open to women without it.

Despite Brannan's lavish spending, though, Calistoga failed to attract the masses and their wealth. The people who moved to the upper Napa Valley—regular families hoping for a place to farm—had no use for Brannan's grandiose plans, but they did need access to basic goods and services. Rather than creating a tourist destination, it turned out that Brannan had founded a town.

He needed, he realized, a general store. He cast about and found just the right man to run it: a Jewish shopkeeper. Henry Getleson, the son of Hessel and Rachel Getleson, was born in Hamburg. Trained as a sculptor, he left Germany when the 1848 riots broke out and sailed to New York City, arriving just as Brannan's newspaper was hyping the golden Sierras.[46]

He soon sailed to Panama, made the difficult passage through the jungle, and finally debarked in San Francisco in March of 1851. He went directly to the gold country. He engaged in general merchandising, starting, most likely, with a wagon or horse bearing wares for the miners. With his corner on the market in the Gold Rush's earliest years, Sam Brannan probably provided the merchandise.

Getleson did well. He came to own his own store in the brand-new city of Shasta, but it burned down when the town did, a common fate for towns and their wooden structures in the days of candles and torchlight. He rebuilt and stayed on until 1863, when he relocated to Placerville, Indiana. He opened a store there, but whatever mining gave the village its name must not have panned out, because Placerville as a town failed to survive. In 1866 he returned to San Francisco, where he intended to take up sculpting again. Sam Brannan had other plans for the adventurous artist.

When Brannan invited Getleson to operate the first general store in Calistoga, Getleson dropped his hammer and chisel and put on his shopkeeper's apron one more time. He teamed up with a Russian Jew named Morris Friedberg. Together they built a wooden 20'x 36' one-story building and opened for business. Like Lazarus and Straus in St. Helena, Getleson and Friedberg also handled the little village's mail. Other storekeepers moved in after Getleson and Friedberg, sensing an opportunity to start businesses on the ground floor of a newly developing community. One of them, a man named Towle, built a building of red brick, a symbol of permanance and thus a good sign that Calistoga might be there to stay, with or without the resort. Towle himself moved on, but the building remained.

Despite their shared religion, Getleson and Friedberg might not have been ideal partners. Russians tended to be more Orthodox than Reform Jews like the ex-sculptor Getleson, and matters of observance were not something most 19th century *Ostjuden* took lightly. The partnership dissolved by mutual agreement within a year. Getleson took on a new business partner, M. Jacobson, and moved across the street to Towle's brick store while Friedberg remained in the old place, with Charles and Fred Friedberg, perhaps his sons, clerking for him.[47]

Getleson interacted very freely with the gentiles in Calistoga. He was among the founding members of the Calistoga Masonic Lodge, established in 1874, and served as its treasurer for many years. He also partnered with two apparent non-Jews named Smith and Brown in a silver mine, the Elephant, on the south side of Kings Canyon in Calistoga. Like most of these small mining enterprises, the Elephant failed to produce much silver.[48]

The post office stayed with Friedberg, but his name does not appear on surviving lists of fraternal orders or other organizations in the small village. This may have been an example of the gap between Reform German Jews, who were more than happy to blend in with the mainstream, and the *Ostjuden*, who worked harder at maintaining their separate Jewish identity.

Ironically, however, it was Friedberg and not the more gregarious Getleson who found a small place in history. A pair of elegant guests visited Morris Friedberg in his country store one warm afternoon. Robert Louis Stevenson had just married the artist Fanny Osbourne, and the couple was looking for a place to honeymoon. According to Stevenson's account in *The Silverado Squatters*, Friedberg (whom he calls "Kelmar") sold them on the notion of sequestering in the abandoned mining town of Silverado, where he once had a branch store, perhaps also with Getleson.

The Kelmar passages are clearly anti-Semitic. The Scottish Stevenson calls Kelmar, a man in his 50s, a "Jew boy," for example, his wife and her friend "jolly Jew girls," and he entitles the chapter in which they appear "With the Children of Israel." Stevenson's mildly satirical style helps to make his characters memorable and endearing: He pokes fun at the vintner Schram, too, for his excessive-seeming hospitality. The characterization of Kelmar, however, as no more than a self-interested, somewhat moronic hawker is hard to swallow. He compounds it with a generalization that hearkens back to the finance-based bias that plagued European Jewry:

> But the Jew store-keepers in California, profiting at once
> by the needs and habits of the people, have made
> themselves in too many cases the tyrants of the rural
> population. Credit is offered, is pressed upon the new
> customer, and when once he is beyond his depth,
> the tune changes, and he is from thenceforth a white
> slave. I believe, even from the little I saw, that Kelmar,
> if he chooses to put on the screw, could send half
> the settlers packing in a radius of seven or eight

> miles round Calistoga. These are continually
> paying him, but are never suffered to get out of debt.
> He palms dull goods upon them, for they dare not refuse
> to buy; he goes and dines with them when he is on an
> outing, and no man is loudlier welcomed; he is their
> family friend, the director of their business and, to a
> degree elsewhere unknown in modern days, their king. [49]

To Stevenson's credit, however, he ultimately gave the shopkeepers his blessing:

> Take them for all in all, few people have done my heart
> more good; they seemed so thoroughly entitled to their
> happiness, and to enjoy it in so large a measure and so
> free from afterthought; almost they persuaded me to be a Jew. [50]

Despite his prejudice, Stevenson was accurate in observing that a disproportionate number of the small mercantile businesses in California were run by Jewish proprietors.

David L. Haas, the Napa merchant, hoped to gain a toe-hold in Brannan's little town. He opened a branch of the Haas Brothers there around 1875 and even dabbled in quicksilver (mercury) mining, an extremely popular and occasionally lucrative pastime for the speculative. The Haases shipped fourteen flasks of the liquidy metal one winter,[51] but it is doubtful that their venture paid off very well. They sold the Calistoga store to a Mr. Beardslee from Lakeport and a few months later, with a great deal of fanfare, opened their new branch in St. Helena.[52]

Henry Getleson passed away in the 1880s. The Friedbergs stayed much longer. Another merchant finally came to take their place and operate the post office: Felix Grauss, whose brother was the town constable. Felix was profoundly German, a fact that would eventually carry him over the brink of disaster.

Chapter Five

During Solomon's lifetime Judah and Israel,
from Dan to Beersheba, lived in safety,
each man under his own vine and fig tree.
                                    —1Kings 5:5

DOWN IN NAPA, FREEDMAN AND DORA LEVINSON WERE ENJOYING
the fruits of their labors. They lived modestly within walking distance of their shop, which had become a fixture on Main Street
despite competition from an increasing number of both Jews and
gentiles. Their children had flourished. The oldest boy, Harry
Levinson, moved to Visalia, where he served as the fire chief and
the town mayor. He was eventually elected to the state legislature.[53]
    Annie Levinson was the oldest girl. Stunningly attractive, she
found her way into San Francisco society, marrying Adolph
Kronberg in 1871. The Kronbergs had six children of their own and
were active members of Temple Emanu-el, the beautifully ornate
synagogue that served as a gathering place for the city's Reform
Jews. Tragically, Adolph died of a heart attack while the children
were still young, leaving Annie nearly destitute. Annie then did
what single Jewish women so often did back in Europe, in the ghettos and *shtetls*: took care of others. She was known for the delicious

chicken soup she delivered to friends and neighbors in need.

The role of women as love bearers and transmitters of news in the Jewish community was essential to the survival of the culture. Even the gossip of *yentas* (busybodies) had its place, for it provided a behavioral rubric within which the members of the group needed to conduct themselves or else face the consequences. Conformity to norms helped promote group stability and deter assimilation.[54]

Annie's sister Sarah Levinson did not marry, nor did she work in a store in Napa. Instead, she also took on the important role of community helper, visiting the sick, spearheading charitable causes and helping to bind together the Jewish families who had come from so far with such diverse backgrounds. Over the years Sarah Levinson made so many doses of chicken soup that she actually wore a dent in the table where she rolled her homemade noodles.

Like a great many Jewish men, Charlie Levinson decided to go into the ready-to-wear clothing industry. He served as a clerk in Abe Levy's Pioneer Clothing Store on Main Street in Napa. Levy eventually moved to Lake County. Charlie Levinson and a friend, the aforementioned St. Helena merchant Alden, opened their own store, Alden and Levinson. After Alden left he joined forces with another friend, Abe Strauss. Eventually Levinson & Strauss became simply Levinson's Clothing Store, and Abe Strauss opened a clothing store specializing in men's wear.[55]

Proud of his Napa roots, Charlie was a founding member of the local Native Sons' chapter. He was its permanent secretary and served the association in that capacity throughout most of his adult life.

He was also an active member of the Unity Volunteer Hose Company. Until 1906, when Napa established a paid fire department, the town depended on its volunteers to put out fires. There was a great deal of competition among the little hose companies. The Reliance, the Alert, and the Unity Hose Companies, the Pioneer Engine Company and Napa Hook and Ladder all raced each other to the scene of a crisis, and the first to get there had access to the closest hydrant. Without television or movies to distract them, large crowds of people ran or rode their buggies or bicycles to watch the heroics of firemen like Charlie. Unity Hose Company was especially noteworthy for the parties it hosted: gaily decorated dances and costume balls complete with dance cards and prizes.

When Unity and the others combined in 1906 to form one city-wide force, Charlie went on to serve as one of the town's first regular fire fighters, while continuing to operate his store.

Charlie Levinson's service with the fire department had a significant and very practical side benefit for Napa's Jewish population. Because of his influence, the Jews of Napa finally had a place to meet, a room on the firehouse's top floor. They convened there for Pesach (Passover) and the Jewish High Holy Days.

Napa's Reform Jews practiced their Judaism quietly and without display during the years around the turn of the century, although sometimes children built little huts out of branches to celebrate Sukkot, the Festival of Booths, which commemorates the fulfillment of God's promise to bring them from the desert to the Promised Land. The Levinsons did not abandon their Judaism, yet nevertheless experienced inclusion within the social center of young Napa. It was a feat that was more possible in the post-Gold Rush American west than in most other places on the planet.

At the urging of his life-long friend Dr. E.Z. Hennessey, Charlie's brother Joe became a pharmacist. Levinson's Pharmacy stood on the southeast corner of Main and First in Napa for decades. Medicine as practiced in the late 19th and early 20th centuries was a far cry from today's health care industry. There were no hospitals in early Napa, no HMOs, no family counselors, no treatment centers. Doctors made house calls and extended credit. Their patients often paid them in goods and services rather than in cash. Pharmacists like Joe frequently worked on a barter basis. Warmly appreciated by many of his peers, they often called him by his nickname, "Pills."

Levinson's Pharmacy had an innovation which no other enterprise in Napa possessed, not even the county infirmary: an X-ray machine. Injured patients and their doctors came to Joe's for an inside look into the mysteries of orthopedics.

Like Sarah, neither Joe nor Charlie married.

It was Clara Levinson whose life path took her the farthest from Napa, at least for a time. While attending one of her Uncle Charlie's Unity Hose Company dances, she met an Englishman, Barnard Levy. Born into a family of cigar manufacturers, Barnie Levy ran away from his boyhood home in London to make his fortune in the New World. He found his way to the gold mining country in Utah, where he acquired a supplier of tobacco and set up a cigar store. He prospered.

Like many young men of the "Gilded Age," he yearned to see San Francisco. It may have been by attending services at the city's famous Temple Emanu-el that he met Annie Levinson Kronberg, who arranged for him to encounter Clara at the dance in Napa. Networking, an essential ingredient to success in business, was also an important feature of matchmaking within the Jewish community.

Barnie and Clara married in 1888 and went to live in Victoria, Canada, where Barnie was a tobacconist until the financial crises of the early 20th century drove him out of business. They retreated to Napa, where he set up a small tobacco shop next to Charlie's clothing store on Main Street.

Barnie Levy never again enjoyed much financial prosperity, but he did not lack for *joie de vivre*. His special interest was music. Sometimes, in San Francisco cabarets, he performed songs he'd written himself.

The Levinsons were thus integral to the commercial infrastructure of Napa. It was a position they shared, as noted earlier, with the Haases. A third important Jewish family whose merchandising efforts greatly benefited the young city were the Schwartzes, five brothers whose last name is variously recorded as Schwarz, Schwartz, Swartz, and sometimes Schwarts.

At least one Schwartz was present in California even before the Gold Rush. A fisherman by that name reportedly sold a barrel of bad (or perhaps just pickled) salmon south of Sacramento to a small group of men who were seeking recruits for the Mexican-American War.[56]

Peter Swartz was listed among the earliest residents of Pope Valley, and a creek there is named for him. H.F. Swartz, perhaps Peter's son, owned a livery and feed store on the corner of Pope and Main Streets in St. Helena in the 1870s that served as the terminus for the stage line to Pope Valley and its Phoenix and Silver Bow quicksilver mines. It is possible that these earlier S(ch)wartzes may have been related to the five brothers, and that their presence attracted the rest.

Herman Schwarz may have been the first of the brothers to open a shop in Napa: a hardware store, established in 1870.[57] He was a "competent tinner" who advertised his competency at roofing, tinning and plumbing. "Doing my own work," he told his customers in 1872, "I can do it cheaper than any one can." He also sold stoves, glass, and fruit cans "at San Francisco prices." Schwarz Hardware was on Main Street, amidst the Levinson and Haas enterprises.[58] The victim of clerical error when he first passed through Ellis Island, Herman was the only brother to spell his name without the "t." He married Lizzie Fleishman in 1871 and had sons named Will, David, and Max. David and William Schwarz built a large home on the corner of Main and Pearl Streets that was demolished in 1936 after being condemned as "too bad to repair." Will took over the administration of the store after his father's death and served as a trustee of the Bank of Napa.[59]

Herman's brother Jake Schwartz relocated to San Francisco for a time and then returned to clerk for many years in the hardware store.

Schwarz Hardware was a favorite hangout for Napa men. Besides paint, carpentry equipment and plumbing supplies (John Golds, a second-generation Napa Jew, ran the plumbing department) Schwarz's sold agricultural equipment, which made it a place where farmers liked to come and exchange gossip, information and news. It also offered a complete line of fishing and hunting gear. Professional hunters dropped by to sell their catch, and locals would gab about the size and abundance of the trout they'd hauled in. Because of their popularity with the voting public, politicians made sure they were in good standing with the Schwarzes.[60]

Brother Henry Schwartz partnered with brother Joseph Schwartz in a dry goods store whose first location was on the ground floor of the Napa Opera House on Main Street. "J&H Schwartz" staged its grand opening shortly before Christmas of 1874, "with a large and varied assortment of goods available for the holiday trade, besides a full line of dry goods, fancy goods, boots, shoes, hats, caps, etc." Henry married Mathilda Weil in 1884 and eventually moved to Santa Paula, California.[61]

Joseph Schwartz may have been the most financially successful of the brothers. He stuck with clothing and dry goods and had shops in several locations, including one that he called the "City of Paris," which probably had some affiliation to the much larger City of Paris store in San Francisco. His wife, nee Adelheide Vogel, had siblings in San Francisco, and her parents were prominent New Yorkers.[62]

The Joseph Schwartzes were so significant socially that the home they built in 1890 made news in the local newspaper. It was a fine Queen Anne/East Lake Victorian on the northeast corner of Oak and Franklin streets in Napa, designed by the popular Napa architect Luther Turton and built by Robert Corlett and Sons. The first floor featured a spacious entrance hall with a wide platform staircase and an airy parlor with a big bay window for watching the comings and goings on the street outside. There was a sitting room as well, and it, too had a bay window. The big (12x16) kitchen had an attached conservatory, and there were four bedrooms upstairs. Even more appealing to the family was the fact that the home had indoor plumbing "and all the modern conveniences," something of a rarity in Napa in 1890, when it was completed.[63]

Joseph bought other lots on the north side of Oak Street, and in 1906 he built an elegant duplex next door to his home on the corner, for the use of his son, David, who rented out the bottom flat to people of import. Theodore Bell, three-time candidate for Governor of California and Napa County's leading politician, lived for a time in the downstairs flat of David Schwartz's duplex.[64]

Finally, brother Max Schwartz taught exercises at the local *Turn Verein*, or athletic club, to members who spoke English. *Turn Vereins* were social and sporting associations popular among German and Swiss men. St. Helena, which was heavily represented with both, also had a *Turn Verein*, and in 1900 Max had the somewhat odd distinction of chairing the Christmas dance there.[65]

Not surprisingly, Max the athlete was a good friend of Charlie Levinson the fireman. Both men belonged to the Odd Fellows (as did Joseph Schwartz). One Thanksgiving Day the Rebekahs (the Odd Fellows' women's auxiliary) held a fancy costume ball at the Opera House that apparently attracted a good portion of the town:

> At an early hour the guests began to arrive, and by eight o'clock the gallery, which was reserved for spectators, was filled to overflowing, their numbers running up to something over two hundred...Max Schwartz, as a traveling photographer, was a source of no little amusement.[66]

Max opened a cigar and liquor store on Main Street near the other Schwar(t)z businesses (the whole block near the Opera House was sometimes called the "Schwarz Block") and later took over the hardware store from his uncle.[67]

There was also at least one Schwartz sister, Emma, who married Hyman Levison of San Francisco in 1871 and had two daughters, Minnie and Helen. Hyman died in 1887 at the age of 41, leaving Emma in the same bind that Annie Levinson Kronberg had experienced. The Levisons, like the Kronbergs, were persons of note (along with the Weils and Vogels) at San Francisco's Temple Emanu-el.

There was also an Isaac Schwartz who lived in Calistoga. His relationship, if any, to the Napa family is unknown. A serious opium addict, he committed suicide in 1892.

The newspaper's society column often covered the Napa Schwar(t)z's comings and goings. Well-heeled friends from San Francisco came often and stayed for weeks, and the Schwartz girls traveled frequently to the city. A small group of twenty of the family's closest friends and relatives gathered to toast Joseph and Adelheide on their 50th anniversary. The guest list included:

> Mrs. and Mrs. Joseph Schwartz, Herman Schwarz, Max
> Schwartz, David Schwarz, Will Schwarz, S. Fleishman,
> Max Schwarz, Lulu Meyer, Mrs. Weil, Florella
> Schwartz, Muriel Schwartz, Mr. and Mrs. Levene,
> Mrs. C. Goldberg, David J. Schwartz, Julius Vogel,
> Minni Levison, Helen Selma Levison, Stella Goldberg.[68]

The Napa newspapers were fascinated with the comings and goings of the prominent family. "It was a late hour," wrote a reporter, "when the guests withdrew, wishing their host and hostess many years of health, happiness and prosperity."

Not all the Jews in Napa City ran stores. One of the most important Napans of Jewish ancestry was Emanuel Manasse, son of a tanner, who came to New York from Frankfurt in 1864. That same year he married a Prussian woman, Amelia Hellwig, whose family were also tanners and probably networked with the Manasses in Europe.

When the Civil War was over, Amelia's brother and father

came to San Francisco and started a tannery at 26th and Mission Streets. Emanuel and Amelia followed soon after, and Emanuel went to work for his in-laws.

Meanwhile, the son of a New Hampshire currier was reviewing the prospects for a life in the wild west. While staying in Napa, French Albert Sawyer, a Christian, noticed that local butchers were discarding sheep pelts with the wool still on them. He bought a pile of pelts and started a small wool-pulling business on the banks of the Napa River, with the help of some Chinese laborers. He soon expanded the operation to include curing the hides themselves, which he and his men pickled in brine and shipped back home along with the wool. Father and son agreed that the prospects for a tanning and wool business in Napa were good. In 1870, B.F. and F.A. Sawyer established the Sawyer Tannery.[69]

They needed an experienced superintendent to help run the place. French Sawyer had met Emanuel Manasse in San Francisco and invited the young German to work for him. Emanuel and Amelia moved to Napa in 1871.

Emanuel Manasse proved to be a brilliant technician. He developed several new methods for tanning sheepskin and buckskin and was able to procure a patent for his ideas. Napa became identified as a source of highest quality leather, and the Sawyer Tanning Company gradually became a major local employer.

The entire Manasse family was involved in the business at least part of the time. Among them was Emanuel's brother Ed, who before joining the tannery worked for the Haas brothers in St. Helena and Calistoga; and Henry J. Manasse, who at the age of twenty-three opened a Napa shoe store on the side to help ride through a downturn in the economy.

Tanning and other aspects of the fur and hide business had long been endeavors in which Jews had engaged, originally interacting with the Vikings. Luxurious and exotic, furs were a delight for the wealthy and a necessity for the cold; and they were portable, another feature of most traditional Jewish enterprises.

Two gentiles who were very important in the fur trade came to the area about the same time Emanuel Manasse did, while their Jewish business partners remained in San Francisco and became leaders at Temple Emanu-el. Gustave Niebaum and John F. Miller, the former a Finnish sea captain and the latter a Civil War general, were principals in the Alaska Commercial Company, along with Louis Sloss, Lewis Gerstle, and A. Wasserman, part of San Francisco's Jewish elite.[70]

Niebaum was captaining a ship in the frigid waters off Alaska in 1867 when the United States acquired the former Russian territory. He sailed into San Francisco harbor with more than half a million dollars worth of seal and otter skins and sold them to Sloss and Gerstle's company, of which he, too, became a partner.

Miller lived in Napa County briefly in the 1850s, when he practiced law and served as county treasurer. He went to San Francisco and was appointed Collector of the Port of San Francisco, a position that introduced him to men like Sam Brannan and other VIPs. He returned to his native Indiana at the start of the Civil War and joined the Union Army as a general. When the war was over he came back to California and fell in with Gerstle, Sloss, Niebaum and the others.

Because of his stature as a war hero, and because he was an American-born gentile with no accent, Miller became the president and main spokesman for the company, while Sloss and the others continued to direct it from behind the scenes. Immediately upon his appointment to the position he went to Washington, DC to negotiate for rights to the fur seal concession in Alaska. This obtained, he then sailed to London and other points around the globe to ensure that the fashion world continued to rely on seal and otter skins for hats, coats and other cold-weather furnishings.

With the money he made in the fur-trading business, Miller was able to build a pillared mansion he named "La Vergne," after a Civil War battlesite where he had distinguished himself. Miller's estate, more beautiful than ever, is now the Silverado Country Club.

Niebaum continued his involvement with the Alaska Commercial Company for the rest of his life, as well. Extremely wealthy, he invested some of his money in what was then a rich man's hobby: the wine business. He became known for his eye for detail and the meticulous care he took in creating his vintages. He was also one of the first to identify that the soil in which the grapes are planted has a direct bearing on the quality of the wine. He built Inglenook, which is today's Niebaum-Coppola Winery. It, too, continues to be one of the Napa Valley's brightest gems.

By 1882, when Niebaum crushed his first vintage, the wine industry had become a prominent part of the county's agricultural life and the most important business north of Yountville. Several Jewish families grew and crushed grapes. The Lazaruses were among the first. Leopold and Julia bought sixteen acres in 1869, planted them in wine grapes, and sold the land a few years later for ten times what they'd paid.[71]

An Oakland man named George Meyers was another who tried his hand as a vintner. In 1883 he crushed some 22,500 gallons of wine on his Mt. Eden ranch two miles east of Oakville.[72]

F.H. Rosenbaum had a small cellar in the basement of his large Victorian home just north of the Beringer Winery. He had made money in San Francisco in the glass business and may have been related to Simon Rosenbaum, one of the few people living in the tiny village of Yountville, just north of Napa, prior to 1880. "Fritz" Rosenbaum is recorded as having made 8,000 gallons in 1885 at his estate, which he named "Johannaberg."[73] Today it is the site of a premium winery, St. Clement.

The Rosenbaums went through some difficult times. Their son August was a heavy drinker. Suffering from alcohol-induced delerium, he wandered from home and died on the side of a road, probably from acute alcohol poisoning.

A Rosenbaum daughter, Bertie, had the scare of her life one evening in 1892. For more than a year, a flamboyant young man calling himself "Count Freyenstine" had been forcing his attentions upon the lovely Bertie, and while at first she may have found this flattering, it finally assumed the form of persecution.[74]

She returned home one night in September after a trip to San Francisco and was warned by her housekeeper that Freyenstine had entered the house in her absence. She dispatched the handyman to get help.

Constable Howard and Officer York, the town night watchman, arrived at the Rosenbaum home quickly. York stationed himself outside a window, lest the phony Count slip out. Bertie lit a candle and led Constable Howard through the big, darkened house, checking room after room. When they were sure no one was on the first floor, they climbed the narrow, twisting staircase and began searching the upstairs, where there were four bedrooms.

The last room was Bertie's. They entered, Bertie with the candle and Howard behind her, and Bertie caught a glimpse of someone beneath the bed. Terrified, she started to run from the room with the candle, leaving the Constable in the dark.

"Set the candle on the stand!" cried Constable Howard. Bertie obeyed and groped her way downstairs through the darkness as quickly as she could.

Howard felt under the bed and found Freyenstine there. He ordered him to stand up and raise his hands. Freyenstine crawled out and pled to be allowed to see "Miss Bertie." He started for the door, but Howard stopped him. The two men struggled and worked their way into the darkened hall, locked in combat.

Suddenly a gun went off. Hearing the shot, Officer York dashed inside from his post beneath the windows and tackled Freyenstine, who was now screaming for "Miss Bertie, Miss Bertie!" York slapped handcuffs on the man and subdued him.

The revolver, it turned out, belonged to Bertie herself. Freyenstine had taken it from her bedside table and was laying in wait for her under her bed with the loaded gun. Somehow he had concealed it from Constable Howard, and in the fray it went off.

Howard and York packed Freyenstine into the police department's horse and buggy and threw him in the St. Helena jail.

The stone *calabozo* (located on grounds now occupied by the St. Helena Parochial School) did not have running water or facilities for food, so one of Constable Howard's jobs was to take the prisoner out to dinner at a nearby restaurant. A few days after the arrest, he was returning the prisoner to his cell after doing just that. Freyenstine asked for permission to clean out the contents of his commode. Howard consented and accompanied him to the door of the jail. He took his eye off the prisoner for just a moment.

Freyenstine dropped the slop bucket and "shot over the back fence like a deer." Before Howard could react, he was gone.

A hue and cry went out for the escaped prisoner. One of the places they sought him was at the home of Henry Lange, a German who ran a laundry in town. Lange had once employed the phony Count. Sure enough, Freyenstine was sitting in Lange's parlor.

When he realized that he had been discovered again, the Count leapt out the window, landing a few feet from one of Howard's officers. He bounded through the bushes and disappeared without a trace. Bertie Rosenbaum spent the next several years terrified that the maniacal Count Freyenstine would return to kill her, as she feared he had intended to do that night.

Bertie Rosenbaum was not the only pretty Jewish girl in St. Helena to have been targeted by an obsessive lover. Minnie Weinberger, her neighbor, suffered an even more devastating blow, one that affected not only the whole town, but St. Helena's most important endeavor, the wine industry

The pre-eminent Jewish couple in the winemaking business before Prohibition was John Weinberger and his wife Hannah, nee Rabbe. The Weinberger family had been candy-makers in Bavaria, and young John entered the trade in 1844 at the age of fourteen. He left Germany in 1848, just as the riots were beginning and it was clear that America held better opportunities for Jews.[75]

From the St. Helena Star, *1878*

From the Napa Journal, *1878*

S(ch)war(t)zes had businesses in the Napa Valley throughout the 19th century and well into the 20th. H.F. Swartz (above, left, St. Helena Star 1874) lived in Pope Valley and was probably unrelated to the Napa S(c)hwar(t)zes. H. S(c)hwarz and J. Schwartz were brothers, despite the different spellings.

Goodman's was the upscale clothing store in St. Helena, circa 1880. Abe Goodman stands in doorway, far right.

St. Helena Star, 6-28-1979 Courtesy of Jack Paulus

Abraham Goodman

Julius Goodman

Jacob Goodman

Freedman Levinson and his son Charlie had stores on Main Street. Charlie (far left in group of four) moved his store's location several times. Freedman (far right above and with the pipe, below) stayed put. His canary (see cage, far left) drew customers.

Dora Levinson, 1884

Henry Getleson and Morris Friedberg were partners first and then competed. Ads are from the Calistogan, *1871 and 1872.*

Emanuel Manasse, photo courtesy of Napa Sawyer Tannery

1885: The management at the Sawyer Tannery. Emanuel Manasse is seated, above #5.

The Haas brothers had stores in Napa (darker building), St. Helena (insert) and Calistoga

Photo courtesy of the Napa Valley Museum

Several Jewish-owned stores lined Main St., Napa in the 1890's. On left, after the bank, are Haas Brothers stationery, Firestine's Shoes, and farther up the street Levinson's Pharmacy.

Photo courtesy of the Western Jewish History Center, Judah L. Magnes Museum

Hartman & Klang, Jewish merchants, set up shop in the Napa Valley town of Rutherford along the County Road (now Highway 29). Other businesses shared the covered wooden sidewalk.

Photo courtesy of the Napa Valley Museum

Charlie Levinson (right, in passenger seat) served in the Napa Fire Department for many years. He was able to reserve a room above the fire station, where Jews convened for High Holidays and other occasions.

Photo courtesy of Claire Erks

The mirror at the back of the store interfered with this rare interior shot of Joe Levinson's pharmacy.

Back row, L-R: Sarah Levinson, Bertha Engle, Lilly Griffith. Middle row, L-R: Minnie Schwartz, Gussie Kather. On floor, L-R: Amelia Kather, Clara Levinson. The pendants on each young woman were given by young men as symbols of affection and intent.

Inside Joe Galewsky's store, St. Helena, 1904.

Photo courtesy of the Napa Valley Museum

He continued as a confectioner in New York City until 1853, when he moved to Indianapolis, Indiana, where he rented a small room at the Union Pacific train depot. There he made sweets to sell to passengers emerging from the trains. A friend described him as "an almost beardless youth. His treasure was his basket of pies."[76]

As his pastry business grew, John rented bigger and bigger rooms, then a whole building and finally bought the entire block. He also procured a twelve-year lease on the lunch and newsstand at the Union depot. He made a modest fortune.

When the Civil War ended in 1865, he bought land and established a nursery and fruit farm. His wife, Anna, whom he may have met in Cincinnati, died the next year, leaving him with a five-year-old daughter, Minnie. Minnie's health was frail, so he began looking for a better climate in which to raise her.

The quest for a healthy environment led him to California and the Napa Valley. In 1870 he liquidated his Indiana assets and bought 100 acres north of the Beringer winery, near the Rosenbaum residence. He built a nice home on a hillside and planted grapes.

He also remarried, this time to Hannah Rabbe, a woman in her thirties from Indiana. They had three children together, the last arriving when Hannah was forty-one.

A contemporary described the Weinberger winery as "large and commodious and equal in convenience to any in the valley."

> The cellar was built of red lava rock in 1876, and the capacity to store is one hundred and fifty thousand gallons. One story is underground for storing wine. Second story [is] for crushing grapes and [a] fermenting house. The building is supplied with fresh spring water from the mountains.[77]

Weinberger made wine, but as a former candy-maker he also became interested in the idea of producing grape syrup, which could be used as a sweet additive in cooking and a substitute for sugar, not unlike corn syrup. He made 1,500 gallons of grape syrup in 1876 and 2,000 gallons the following year.

Like Leopold Lazarus, John Weinberger enjoyed a good deal of popularity with his fellow citizens, especially those in the wine industry. He was a founding member of the St. Helena Viticultural Club and served as its treasurer. His honesty and integrity were impeccable: He was the first in the Valley, for example, to reveal that the phylloxera louse had invaded the region and had already manifested itself in his vineyard.[78]

Weinberger's productive, vigorous life came to an abrupt and violent end in 1882, when his youngest child was a year old. An employee named William Gau had become obsessed with Minnie Weinberger, who was then twenty-one. Weinberger (and perhaps Minnie) opposed the man's involvement in her life.[79]

The vintner was at the Barro (Lodi Lane) railroad stop in St. Helena shortly before noon on a March day, perhaps waiting for a delivery. Gau stepped off the train and approached him on the platform and may have said a few words. He then reached into his overcoat pocket, pulled out a pistol and held it to Weinberger's face. He pulled the trigger, waited two or three seconds and fired again, then fired a third time five seconds after that.

E.M. York, who lived nearby, witnessed the event and held Weinberger's hand as he lay dying. It was all over in about ten minutes.

Weinberger's murder was an outrage that shocked the community. Gau was arrested and was to be tried by a jury of Weinberger's peers that included his closest friends in the wine industry: Charles Krug, Jacob Beringer, C.T. McEachran, John Thomann, William Castner, Ed Heymann and others. The only concession to Gau's needs was that the trial would be conducted in German, which also happened to be the language of Krug, Beringer, Thomann (a Swiss), Heymann and possibly Castner. Rather than be subjected to the noose at someone else's hand, Gau did the work himself, committing suicide before the trial commenced.

Weinberger's wife Hannah took over the winery. In 1889 the Paris World's Fair honored her work as a vintner with a silver medal, the first ever to be awarded to a woman from California. With three young children still at home, it was an impressive feat of courage and tenacity.

Elsewhere, other Jews were also attracting attention in the 1880s, for very different reasons...

Chapter Six

I will assemble the exiles.
—Micah 4:6

JEWS BEGAN COMING TO AMERICA IN GREATLY INCREASING NUMBERS
in 1871, when a bloody pogrom in Odessa on the Romanian border
began a migration from southern Russia.[80] Some 30,000 Jews fled
Russia for the United States in the 1870s. The following decade
saw more pogroms as the garrote of anti-Semitic oppression tight-
ened. Czar Alexander II had been more or less friendly to the Jews,
but his reactionary successor, Alexander III, was not. Alexander
III's "May Laws," passed in May 1881, required Jews within the
Pale of Settlement to leave their small towns and cram into pre-
scribed areas within the larger cities.[81] When governments around
the world protested this inhumanity, Alexander replied that the
Jews had been exploiting the Christian population. Most saw
through this. Many tried to help the Russian Jews escape the persecution by paying for their passage to safety. Hebrew Aid Societies
sprang up in several places around the world.

   With their life's treasures in bags or bound in blankets and
slung over their shoulders, some 25,000 Russian Jews stepped off

the boat onto Ellis Island in 1881-82.[82] This was just the beginning. Almost 600,000 arrived in the United States between 1881 and 1900.[83] Frightened yet hopeful faces long confined within tiny, cramped enclaves now looked upon a wide-open continent where they, like the Sephardic and German Jews before them, were free to live and work and move about at will. Emma Lazarus wrote a poem contrasting the Colossus of Rhodes, an ancient symbol of power and might, with the statue greeting these stricken refugees. Some of its lines are among the best-known verses in American literature:

> Not like the brazen giant of Greek fame
> With conquering limbs astride from land to land;
> Here at our sea-washed, sunset gates shall stand
> A mighty woman with a torch, whose flame
> Is the imprisoned lightning, and her name
> Mother of Exiles. From her beacon-hand
> Glows world-wide welcome; her mild eyes command
> The air-bridged harbor that twin cities frame,
> "Keep, ancient lands, your storied pomp!" cries she
> With silent lips. "Give me your tired, your poor,
> Your huddled masses yearning to breathe free,
> The wretched refuse of your teeming shore,
> Send these, the homeless, tempest-tossed to me,
> I lift my lamp beside the golden door!"

The most effective Jewish philanthropist of this era was Baron Maurice de Hirsch, descendant of a family of court bankers and husband of the equally philanthropic Clara Bischoffsheim de Hirsch. Concerned that the new refugees were subject to poverty as well as induction into radical causes like anarchism and Communism, the de Hirsches poured $2.4 million into educational, vocational and relocation programs.[84]

The de Hirsches and a like-minded philanthropist who followed them, Jacob Schiff, felt that freeing Jews from centers of dense population like New York and Chicago would enable them to more readily blend in. They assisted the new arrivals (most of them

Russian) in setting up agricultural communities in sparsely populated areas of North and South America. Schiff formulated a plan to use Galveston, Texas, as an alternative to Ellis Island as a port of entrance. The Galveston Plan was intended to facilitate the newcomers' dispersal to the interior.

The first agricultural settlement for Russian Jewish transplants was in Catahoula Parish, Louisiana, not far from the Mississippi River in the eastern part of the state. A flood swept away everything in 1882—their houses, their crops, their livestock, and all of their equipment—forcing most (but not all) to move to San Antonio, St. Louis and other places.

The Friedman family was one who sampled farming life through the auspices of Baron de Hirsch. Cordial makers in Russia, they went to a place called Devil's Lake, North Dakota in the 1880s.[85] Prairie fires and the drought of 1884-85 made it no place to resurrect the cordial business, let alone rest contented under their own vine and fig tree. They moved to Chicago, where son Herman Friedman worked at the California Wine Company, which he owned along with other members of the family. The company imported wine grapes from California for the local Italian and Greek immigrants to press into their own homemade vintages. Around 1904 Herman sent his wife and two children back to Russia to live with her parents while he completed medical school, and when he was done the reunited family moved to the small city of Rock Island, Illinois, where he launched his career as a doctor.[86] Herman's grandsons Alan Steen, MD and Art Finkelstein would also become very familiar with California grapes, a century later.

Ekiel and Mindel Bronfman also tried to scratch a living from the hard-to-work high plains in Wapella, a town that would later be part of the province of Saskatchewan. Like the Friedmans, they didn't stay there long; their son Sam would build an empire from their new home base in Montreal.[87] The Bronfman family would eventually have a big impact on the Napa Valley, as well.

The de Hirsches' relocation idea had fatal flaws. Few former *shtetl* dwellers were emotionally or culturally equipped for the isolation of farm life, and taming the American interior was an overwhelming challenge. Flood, drought, fire and disease chased away would-be gentile ranchers, too. The Galveston Plan was also conceptually flawed. The extra travel time to Texas meant increased fares and a longer voyage, a hardship for the already poor, and once they arrived the immigrants still faced an arduous and expensive trek to destinations that could have been reached quicker and cheaper by going through New York. Reform Jews like the de Hirsches and Schiff, while true lovers of humanity and advocates of their fellow Jews, may not have been fully aware of the needs of the urban Orthodox, and Russians émigrés were almost always that.

Despite the exodus to the US (as well as to South America, South Africa and Australia) some 6,000,000 Jews remained in Russia, by far the most reactionary and least progressive of the world's major powers. The entire working class suffered from repressive conditions, and since the Jews were on the bottom of the power chain, they were the most often abused. When anti-monarchist resentments threatened to boil over, the Romanov czars sat back and watched the gentiles maul the Jews to let the steam out.

While anti-Semitic violence was heating up in Russia, new forms of liberalism were also developing, with ideas that went farther than those of the post-Napoleonic reform movement. Socialism and its extreme expression, Communism, occupied the thoughts and conversations of many in the *shtetls*, as well as in the universities and on the streets. It was Russian students—impressionable, energetic and unhindered by a sense of their own mortality—who proved to be the richest soil for planting seeds of revolution.

To provide a diversion for its unhappy young men (and to

retake Port Arthur, which had been attacked), Russia declared war on Japan. It would be quick and easy payback, hoped the new czar, Nicholas II, and it would showcase Russia's strength to the world as well as to dissident Russians. With Japan disposed of, China and her riches beckoned, an extra benefit.

There were, however, no more than 80,000 troops in Russia. Five thousand miles and the winter of 1905 stood between St. Petersburg and Port Arthur. Undeterred, Nicholas and his generals conscripted men from Russia and her territories to become soldiers.

One of these was a young Jew named Albert Eugene Kufflevitch, who worked as a deliverer for his father's meat market in Warsaw. Al was yanked from his parents' home to serve in the quartermaster's corps, where he and a few others were sent out ahead of the Russian Army to find and prepare supplies for the hordes to follow. Following the route of the uncompleted Trans-Siberian Railway, he used government-issued rubles to buy food and other necessities from farmers and merchants along the way.[88]

It was a long, brutal trip, made mostly on foot. By the time Al and two companions arrived at Port Arthur, the war was all but lost, and the Motherland was on the brink of revolution. With a small fortune in rubles and supplies at their disposal, Al and his friends faced a decision: whether to return to the pogroms and the long walk back across Siberia, or to board one of the American destroyers harbored at Port Arthur and pay for protection with government funds. Quite naturally, they chose the latter.

One of the men was discovered and removed from the ship (and probably executed on the spot). The ship pushed off with Al and his remaining friend safely concealed, and eventually they arrived in San Francisco, where they parted ways.

Al found work in a butcher shop in the foggy city and set about to making a new life as "Al Kaufman," a good name to hide behind lest the Russians came hunting for him and their missing rubles. A dashing, daring newcomer to the Jewish community could not go unnoticed for long. His unconventional life path would soon cross that of another, equally unconventional life.

William Wolff Biber (aka Bieber) had been a jeweler and a rabbi in New York City, where a tidal wave of Jewish immigrants was washing ashore. The Bibers had five children, four girls and an older boy, and it was the boy, Gesa, whose success was helping Wolff's family rise above the swarming mass of newcomers. Gesa was a gifted composer who played the zimbalon, a kind of dulcimer favored by gypsies in Hungary, the family's country of origin. Gesa had become, at a young age, the director of the orchestra at the elegant Waldorf-Astoria, a spectacular achievement for an immigrant family.

Tuberculosis, the plague of 19th century, ended his career, however, and the family moved to Denver, where the air was purer. Aware of his talent, a group of doctors' wives invited Gesa to play for a social event while he was recovering. Seeing a chance to regain the esteem he had enjoyed in New York, Gesa gladly consented, but during a rehearsal he suffered a hemorrhage and died.

Without its star performer the family drifted west, all the way to San Francisco, where the girls (Doris, Anna, and Martha—the fourth, Bella, was blind) became vaudeville actors. Calling themselves the "Biehle Sisters," these miniature performers sang, danced and told jokes on the little stages of small towns in the greater Bay Area under their father's close supervision and management.

Doris Biber, the oldest, soon met Al Kaufman. It was a union of two high-spirited risk-takers, too adventurous to settle for the mundane life of a butcher business. When the city of San Francisco was destroyed in 1906, Al and Doris took to the road.

Had the Gold Rush still been alive, there's little doubt but that the Kaufmans would have found a place for themselves somewhere in the heart of it. What happened instead was that Al was lured by another vision of romance and adventure: to become a cowboy.

He quickly found work with an Italian ranching family, the Naves of Novato. Ranch life suited the Kaufmans well, and it was-

n't long before they wanted a spread of their own, an idea so
absolutely unattainable in their countries of origin that had they
uttered such a wish they would have been ridiculed, or worse.

Times, however, were hard, money was tight, and riding the
range didn't pay well. One day while the couple was pondering
how to amass the capital to buy the ranch of their dreams, a peddler
happened by—a Jewish one, of course.

Inspired, Al became a peddler, too. His specialty was furniture,
a heavy item as far as peddling was concerned, but the trans-
Siberian trek and Al's brief career with the Naves had put muscle
on his bones. Loading his horse-drawn wagon with furnishings
from farm families desperate for money, he then auctioned off the
goods to San Franciscans, many of whom were newly arrived Jews
from Eastern Europe who had come via New York and didn't mind
a few nicks and dings.

The process worked well. Soon Al and Doris were able to rent
a small store in what was then the little saloon town of Vallejo.
They sold second-hand furniture to the families of Mare Island
workers, a market whose numbers increased steadily as the facility
landed contracts to build medium-sized ships for the US Navy.
Thus began the Vallejo Furniture Store, in the heart of the red light
district.

The Kaufman family was also expanding. The year 1909 saw
the birth of their daughter, Rozaline, a fair-haired little ball of energy. Talented like her mother's side of the family and adventurous
like her father's, friendly, intelligent Rozaline demonstrated her
entrepreneurial wisdom early. When the great influenza epidemic
struck in 1918, and everyone was forced to wear gauze masks, she
invested what little money she had in gauze, lace, and sequins and
made fancy coverings for the mouths of the local madams.

Also living in Vallejo was Isadore Meyer, who had grown up
in San Francisco and fled with his family to Vallejo when the earthquake and fire leveled the city. Isadore had a pawn shop called the
"City Loan Office" on Georgia Street. By 1919 his business had

prospered enough for him to deal in new goods, and the City Loan Office became Meyers Jewelers. He married Lena Bellingko, a Russian immigrant whose family was in the furniture business (Bellings Furniture Company) in Oakland, and they had two sons, Benton and Wesley. The Kaufmans and the Meyers joined the congregation that was forming in Vallejo. Young Wesley Meyer would one day follow in his father's footsteps.

One advantage to living in or close to the Napa Valley was that the wine was exceptional, even before World War I. Jewish vintners like the Rosenbaums and Weinbergers were accepted and even celebrated in the Napa Valley, but Jewish middlemen were not. Morris Estee, who operated the Hedgeside Winery near today's Silverado Country Club and ran unsuccessfully for governor of California, was criticized for spending too much time with "foreigners," especially Emanuel Goldstein, a wine merchant. The complaint was thinly veiled anti-Semitism, a sentiment that was increasing in America as the numbers of Jewish Eastern Europeans started to swell.[90]

Ferdinand Haber was Gustave Niebaum's marketing representative and one of the secrets behind Inglenook Winery's considerable success. As an employee of Alfred Greenbaum & Co., Haber managed to have Niebaum's wines served at private clubs and other elite settings back east and kept out of lower echelon restaurants, which was where most California wines went around the turn of the 20th century when they arrived on the East Coast. The American wines that received the most attention, especially in New York, were those manufactured in New York state and in the Mississippi Valley. Inglenook's success in Manhattan surely irked some of its competitors.[91]

The main target of the local vintners' objections was a cartel of major San Francisco wine merchants who pooled their resources and became the California Wine Association (CWA). Jewish financiers Isaias Hellman and Benjamin Dreyfus bankrolled it.

Individual vineyard-owners and small wineries sold their production to the CWA, which blended and stored the juice in a central cellar and huge, 2,000,000 gallon capacity warehouse in San Francisco. Other wine storage facilities were scattered about the Bay Area. Henry Lachman, who had an outstanding palate, oversaw the blending and fermenting process.

By 1902, the CWA controlled more than fifty wineries, including many in the Napa Valley, and while at first it was the smaller wineries like Vine Cliff whose output it received, larger ones began to fall under its spell. Oakville's Brun & Chaix, aka the French American Winery, had a large market share in Jewish-friendly New Orleans and was one of the best known to attract the CWA's interest. The massive Uncle Sam Winery on the Napa River was another, as was the Tubbs' Hillcrest Winery in Calistoga. Greystone, the biggest of all in storage capacity, also went to the CWA.

In truth, small vintners did have something to fear from the CWA. In controlling as much volume as it did (84% of the state's total wine production),[92] it could afford to pay more for grapes than independent vintners could, and it could charge less for its wine. Growers and consumers benefited, but many independent vintners found the CWA to be more than they could handle. With the devastating infestation of the phylloxera louse, the high shipping rates charged by the Southern Pacific Railroad and competition from the wine cartel, few wineries made much money at all in the years leading up to Prohibition.

The 1906 earthquake and fire destroyed the CWA's San Francisco facility. The following year they built an enormous and expensive winery at Point Richmond, near Benicia. "Winehaven" was a three-story brick-and steel castle with turrets and crenellated parapets that overlooked San Pablo Bay like a fortress on the Rhine. Inside, it was a technological masterpiece for its day, with special sidings for railcars, a 50-ton crusher that discharged a ton-and-a-half of grapes a minute, a fully automated pumping and blending system, and a machine-operated bottling line. There was nothing like it anywhere else in America.

The CWA was so dominant a presence that at one of its facilities near Fresno a town sprang up: Calwa, which still exists today, although its population is less than 800.

One of the many advantages that Hellman and company enjoyed was access to a network of well-placed wine merchants, many of them Jewish, throughout the country. Like Haber for Inglenook, CWA representatives were able to ensure that their wines did not receive second-class treatment from East Coast restaurateurs and retailers. Among the most common of these slights was the practice of pouring good California wines into bottles with French labels and charging more for it. The CWA itself sometimes combated this practice by purposely mislabeling some of its wine as French, presumably in response to those who had done it to them.

Not only did many wineries resent the California Wine Association; so did non-aligned wine merchants. The most important of these was Lachman & Jacobi, allied Jewish families whose winery and distribution network had been among the first in the Central Valley. (The Lachman family thus had branches in both camps.) One of the independent merchants' biggest objections was that the CWA was partial to wines of the Napa Valley and thus gave them certain advantages.[93]

The CWA approached its competition from all angles, including above. Lobbies for the group saw to it that Congress passed laws restricting the use of sugar in the fermentation process. The addition of sugar was a necessary practice for winemakers in New York state and the midwest, where the growing season was shorter. The competition now had to pay additional taxes on their product.

The CWA played hardball. Its aggressive strategies differed from those engaged in by another hardball liquor merchandising group, the Royal Arch Masons, who were loosely affiliated with the Masons but mainly Catholic (although some Jews also belonged to the Royal Arch.) Royal Archers from Napa County were known to strong-arm restaurateurs into carrying certain brands of local wine and not others.

It was not competition from small independents, local rough-necks or midwestern wineries that proved to be the CWA's undoing. All the while the cartel was jockeying to stay in the lead in the wine industry, another, darker horse was approaching from behind. Prohibition, a movement dear to the heart of many Protestants, dried up the alcoholic beverage industry in January 1920.

As World War I drew American doughboys across the sea and the storm clouds of Prohibition gathered, certain citizens demonstrated an emotion that was all too familiar to recent Jewish immigrants: xenophobia, with scapegoating.

(Part Two)

Chapter Seven

There is no cluster of grapes to eat,
None of the early figs that I crave.
—Micah 7:1

HEAVILY POPULATED WITH GERMAN IMMIGRANTS, THE NAPA REGION
had a problem when World War I broke out: how to express loyal-
ty to the correct side. The wine industry was the Valley's major
claim to fame and the source of its greatest wealth. It had come to
depend on allusions to Rhenish castles like Winehaven and
Beringer Brothers' Rhine House for much of its ambience and
appeal. The more popular the idea of Prohibition grew and the less
acceptable Germany seemed, the less savory and the less salable
the Valley's principal product became.

On January 6, 1916, the *Napa Daily Journal* printed an article
from the *American Review of Reviews* that praised Germany's sea
power as "unbreakable" and her military position as "practically
invincible." The very next day it reported that the US Navy was
considering abandoning Mare Island "because its channel was
inadequate." Its hand thus slapped, the paper never again praised
things Teutonic.[1]

On the contrary. The newspapers of Napa County became enthusiastically ultra-patriotic, ready to reveal the "seditions" of any who spoke ill of America or well of the Kaiser. Freedom of Speech, both in journalism and in private life, suffered a sudden and dramatic death in the Napa Valley. One who learned this the hard way was Felix Grauss, who had run the post office in Calistoga for sixteen years and was now just assistant postmaster due to the presence of Woodrow Wilson in the White House, the first Democrat since Grover Cleveland.

Perhaps smarting from his demotion to assistant, Grauss was heard making grumpy comments critical of America's involvment in the war. Especially damning was his opinion that the Liberty Loan drive to sell bonds to finance the war was "worthless." Liberty Bonds were sold at the post office.

In the frenzied patriotism that was whipping the populace into a froth for war, such utterances could not be tolerated. A mob of more than twenty men calling themselves the "committee of safety" grabbed Grauss and four others in the dark of the night and hauled them to the Calistoga city hall, where all five men were forced to kiss the American flag. Complaints about this injustice would have been difficult, because the leaders of the group were the Sheriff of Napa County and the District Attorney.[2]

Several of Grauss's friends heard about the debacle and ran to vouch for him, and he was released. Two weeks later, however, Calistogans overheard Arnold Kosch, J.C. Lebner and P. Siebreight speaking German. They called the police, who arrested the trio "for their own protection."[3]

The stubborn Grauss repeated his comments about the Liberty Bonds. The new postmaster overheard, fired him, and saw to it that he was also removed from his other civic involvement, the elections committee. A grand jury quickly indicted Grauss for violating the Espionage Act. Finally, an agent for the US Secret Service went to Calistoga and determined that Grauss was, indeed, pro-German and arrested him.

Within a week of the grand jury report (in October, 1918) the name of another immigrant, August Lutge, appeared on the front page of the *Journal* along with a petition declaring him and his wife to be "undesirable citizens" because they refused to contribute to the Liberty Bond in Napa. Among the twenty-six men who signed the declaration of the Lutges' undesirability were three Jewish businessmen who should have known better: E.G. Manasse, Will Schwarz (son of Herman) and W. Bamburg, of the fashionable Bamburg's clothing store in Napa.[4]

Viewed from a broad perspective, Felix Grauss was lucky he lived in Calistoga and not Eastern Europe. The French Ambassador to Russia reported that Jews in Poland and Galicia who were suspected of being pro-German were being snatched from their homes and hung. With the Kaiser's army at their doorstep, the Poles let loose a series of savage pogroms against their Jewish population that resulted in the obliteration of whole communities. Cut off by the war from fleeing to the west, hundreds of thousands of Jews bundled up their possessions and moved east, into the heart of Russia.[5]

A quarter million Jews entered the Russian army, mainly by conscription, to fight in World War I. They trudged off to face the Austrians when the latter invaded Poland in the summer of 1914. As Russia pressed into the Austrian province of Galicia, however, the Germans pushed into Russia's Polish provinces. The Russian and Austro-Hungarian armies wrestled each other for several months on the soil of Austrian Poland, but it was the Austrians who prevailed.

The Czar called for an infusion of troops to reinforce the failing Russian front, opening the ranks of the army to students. Students, however, were the most willing to listen to voices of discontent. Socialist, Communist and anarchistic organizers, many of them non-practicing Jews, worked among the young recruits and found sympathizers. Their message was anti-war. *Direct your ener-*

gy against the Establishment, said the Bolshevik Lenin and the Menshevik Trotsky; *turn away from the international struggle and toward a civil war between the classes throughout Europe.*

Strikes ensued. By the end of 1916 many Russian soldiers were throwing down their arms and hailing the agitators.

In March of 1917, the Czar abdicated and fled to a remote chateau in the forest, ending a succession of mostly anti-semitic Romanov royalty who had ruled since the 17th century. A provisional government tried to guide the new Russian Republic through the resulting social and political chaos while it continued to press the war, but after six turbulent months, the Republic failed, and the floodgates opened. The Bolsheviks seized the Kremlin, and just as American war frenzy was at its height, Russia withdrew completely from World War I. In July 1918, Czar Nicholas II and his family were murdered at their family retreat.

For a while, many Jews around the world cheered this turn of events, hoping that without the Czar there would be safety for their brethren in Eastern Europe. This sentiment was difficult for most Americans to understand. Without a clear sense of the horrors that had been wreaked upon Jewry for centuries under the Romanovs, American gentiles tended to romanticize the royal family.

As demonstrated above, anyone who opposed the war was, to the average American, an enemy and a potential saboteur of democratic government. Thus many looked upon newly arrived, leftist sympathizing Eastern European Jews as a potential menace to America. The labor unions that they peopled and helped to found were alarming, as were the social/benevolent *Arbeiter Rings* (Workmen's Circles), which often had strong Socialist and even Communist messages.[6]

Ninety percent of the Jews in America now lived in cities, fully two-thirds of them in Manhattan, which was the heart of the heavily Jewish garment industry. The International Ladies Garment Workers Union (ILGWU) and other organizations with a large proportion of Jews in their membership staged strikes against conditions in the needle workers' sweatshops.[7]

Few middle-class rural Americans sympathized with the concept of strikes or understood the needs of the strikers. Especially repugnant to the Napa Valley establishment was the IWW, the Industrial Workers of the World (aka "Wobblies"), whose revolutionary approach to unionism had special appeal to low-wage workers in the textile and mining industries. Quicksilver mining in Napa County was enjoying a renaissance because of the metal's many wartime uses.[8] Wobblies were therefore considered locally dangerous. They opposed entrance into the war, which made them all the more unsavory to people in the Napa Valley.

Unaware of how free America really was, some of the new immigrants did in fact pose a mild threat. The IWW was not benign. In 1919 an IWW-related anarchist plot to assassinate prominent men resulted in bombings in several American cities. Many of the suspects came from the Squirrel Hill area in Pittsburgh, home to a large Russian-Pole population. Among the Pittsburgh residents alive to witness these events was Reuven Katz, who had emigrated from South Africa, where he ran a ginger beer factory. His grandson, Reuben Katz, would eventually find his way to the Napa Valley under far more peaceful circumstances.

The "Red Scare" that the bombings prompted further soured many American gentiles to Jews. Thus when Karl Alberti, an immigrant living in St. Helena, was arrested for making seditious comments, the *St. Helena Star* revealed that he had been under suspicion for a while. Police found IWW and other "anarchistic literature" in his room and vowed that even if he were found innocent of wrong-doing, he would be persuaded not to live within the city limits.[9] Max Jasnau, a Wobbly with a tailoring business on Main Street in Napa, was not only accused of sedition but of molesting two small girls.[10]

In the Napa Valley, then, anyone who opposed America's

involvement in World War I—whether by supporting the Germans outright or sympathizing with the IWW or the Communists—came under attack. Three weeks after the Grauss affair, the lead judge of the Napa Superior Court, Henry Gesford, declared at a public rally that utterers of seditious statements shouldn't kiss the flag—they should be shot.[11]

The hawkish Judge Gesford was not really anti-Semitic; he partnered in a San Francisco law firm with Henry G.W. Dinkelspiel, son of businessman and noted philanthropist Moses Dinkelspiel, a founding member of Temple Emanu-el. The Jews with whom Gesford was most familiar were Reform businessmen and professionals who were as wary of Communists as he was. With the tidal wave of impoverished *Ostjuden* who had washed upon American shores for the past three decades, though, Reform Jews had become a minority. The new non-assimilating, urban-grown Orthodox contingent seemed strange to most Californians and to many Reform Jews, as well.

Another area where Reform and Orthodox Jews differed was in the subject of Zionism, the quest for a Jewish national homeland. Reform Jews (and thus most of California's Jewry) were generally cool to Zionism, hoping not to reorganize in a Jewish nexus but rather to interact fully with the gentile majority. Viennese journalist Theodore Herzl helped to found the modern Zionist movement in 1897.[12] Louis Brandeis, a Boston attorney who would become a Supreme Court Justice, was among those who helped spur on the movement in America in the years around World War I. Argentina, Uganda, Madagascar, Cyprus, the Dakotas and Palestine were among the locations considered for the new Zion. The latter may have seemed the logical choice, for it was the site of the original Holy Land, but it was part of the Ottoman Empire, and the Turks were not especially amenable to the idea of giving it away.[13]

When Great Britain in its "Balfour Declaration" of 1917 announced that it favored the Jewish repopulation of Palestine, many Jews rejoiced, unaware that this pronouncement was little more than a public relations ploy to win Jewish support toward the war effort. The Turks were part of the Central Powers, allied with Germany. When the war ended in 1918 and the victorious countries carved up the land of the defeated, Palestine fell to the apparently Jewish-friendly Great Britain.[14] Many young people left their European ghettos and migrated there. They drained swamps and irrigated the desert. The land responded and began to bear.

Not long after, however, Britain issued a series of "White Papers" reversing its support of Palestine as a Jewish homeland. As the world shifted from horse power to horsepower, oil had become increasingly important. There was no oil in Palestine, but its neighbors—Muslims, like the Turks—had it in abundance. No longer needing Jewish support, Great Britain all but shut the door on the Zionists, and the Arabs, Britain's sweethearts after all, entered into fabulously lucrative business ventures with English-speaking oil moguls.

Upper- and upper-middle-class Americans of the era were usually Anglophiles. After the "White Papers," American anti-Semitism became painfully obvious. In 1921, 1924 and 1929, patrician Congressmen passed immigration laws similar to those it had applied against Asians in the prior century. It was getting much more difficult for Emma Lazarus' huddled masses to see the mighty woman with the torch.

A young Hungarian named Zoltan Rosenberger had already had a chance to become an American. In 1913 his mother had sailed to New York with him and his two sisters to investigate the prospects for moving to the New World. While she was laying out the preliminary groundwork, however, Europe erupted into World War I. Zoltan's father, Farkas, wrote to them insisting they all return. They did, but just behind them was the Romanian army, which churned through the prune orchards of the surrounding countryside and conquered their hometown, changing its name from

Cluj Napoca to Kolozsvar. Harsh laws were instituted, including one forbidding the citizens from speaking Hungarian anymore.[15]

Zoltan longed to get away—to be an adventurer, if not in America, then in a tropical locale like the jungles of the Amazon. His mother and older brother nixed the jungle plan, but they wrote to relatives in Los Angeles hoping to arrange shelter and a job for him. The quota system had just come into effect, though, and Zoltan's chances of going to the United States any time soon were slim. He was, moreover, about to turn eighteen, when he would have to register for the dreaded Romanian army. In a hurry, his Los Angeles contacts found him a connection in Mexico, and he booked passage for Vera Cruz.

Aided by photographs that Zoltan's mother had mailed them, a Russian Jewish couple met the young man at the steamy Mexican seaport. They owned and operated a small candy-making business, but Zoltan couldn't speak Spanish, and they refused to take him in. They sent him to Hungarian friends in Mexico City who owned a Cadillac dealership, but once again his lack of Spanish prevented him from landing a job. The Jewish networking system that had helped Jews survive the persecutions of centuries was failing young Zoltan.

His funds nearly gone and his optimism severely challenged, he finally found his way to Sonora in the Mexican northwest, where he joined a group of Jewish men who were peddling merchandise to miners. He went on foot, partnering with a Mexican who carried the load on his back. They sold men's clothing and whatever else he and his assistant could carry. Mexico, however, proved to be no more stable than Hungary. A revolution closed down his merchandise supplier, and his peddling business went under.

He went elsewhere and started again, but just as he was getting ready to collect on the credits he had extended to the miners at this new location, the Mexican stock market crashed and the mine shut down. His clientele vanished, and his pockets stayed empty.

Nearly penniless, he and a close peddler friend went to

Nogales to work for a mattress manufacturer who had a store in Los Mochis, some 400 miles away. They shipped mattresses from the factory to the store. It was hard, hot, backbreaking, spirit-crushing work—the same kind of hard labor that Jewish men had endured in the Sierras nearly a century earlier. Zoltan Rosenberger's goal of peace beneath the vine and fig tree seemed a long way from being realized.

Unfortunately, the valley that would someday be described as an Eden was busy dealing with devils. Feeding on the xenophobia that had been inflamed by World War I, the Invisible Empire of the Ku Klux Klan, a fraternal organization of white Protestant men, sought recruits in rural areas. Two thousand spectators watched two hundred Klansmen ignite a 20' cross on a field near Napa State Hospital in 1923.[16] This was just a foretaste of the KKK rally held in St. Helena in 1924, where between 8,000 and 10,000 witnessed the Klan's burning cross and heard them preach hatred toward African Americans, Mexicans and Jews.[17] The KKK's appeal in the Valley may have been somewhat impeded by the fact that it also opposed Catholics and alcohol, the former comprising a substantial part of the population and the latter continuing to be manufactured and consumed on the sly despite Prohibition, which put an end to the alcoholic beverage business in 1920. The KKK was popular enough, however, to send chills up the spines of many. Some of the Jews who had stayed despite the collapsing economy now packed their things and moved away.

Quite a few residents, including at least one of the remaining Jews, went into the bootlegging business during Prohibition. Joe Yudnich, a Polish-born rancher who was probably the only remaining Jew in Pope Valley, was included in a round up of illicit booze merchants that involved a number of well-known citizens.[18]

Theodore Bell, the Democratic politician who lived for a while in David Schwarz's flat, spoke out strongly against Prohibition. He spearheaded important but unsuccessful litigation intended to undo the amendment in California. (He may also have been involved with a group of conscientious objectors, who retained him as an attorney. When the apparent association became public, he was threatened with disbarment.)

It has been speculated that Bell participated in a major boot-legging ring, perhaps a network that reached as far as Canada and the spirits manufacturer Sam Bronfman, who ran Joseph Seagrams & Sons Distillery. Bronfman accommodated American drinkers with illegal shipments of his product. The *St. Helena Star* reported on a social event that Bell held at his home where the guest list included some local and state politicians and several San Francisco officials who were in a position to abet a large bootlegging enter-prise. Also present were some of Bell's local Jewish friends. Julius and Jake Goodman, the sons of Abraham Goodman, were there. They now operated their father's department store.

Joe Galewsky was at the party, too. All grown up now, Joe ran the St. Helena post office from his popular stationery/bookstore. Both Emanuel and Joe Galewsky had involved themselves with the Democratic party. Afflicted with asthma and tuberculosis, Emanuel had nevertheless landed an internship working for the state Judiciary Committee in its San Francisco office, and in 1884 he was a delegate to the state Democratic convention in Stockton. He supervised operations at St. Helena's bonded wine warehouse beginning with Grover Cleveland's administration and was still at the helm there under a Republican in 1904 when his diseases final-ly felled him.[19] Joe, the prankster, picked up the political gauntlet his half-brother had dropped. He was appointed postmaster of St. Helena during Wilson's presidency, a position he would again enjoy in 1936 when the next Democrat, Franklin Roosevelt, came into office.

It does not appear that either Emanuel or Joe observed their Judaism very closely. Like the Levinsons in Napa, they were both very active in the Native Sons of the Golden West. The St. Helena

The Industrial Removal Office attempted to disperse Jews from eastern urban areas to various locations around America. Even Napa was, literally, "on the map," although there is no record of IRO activities here. Shown above, the western United States in Yiddish, courtesy of Jack Roth, Legendary Graphics.

Rozaline Kaufman took the stage as a dancer and a singer. She won awards as a violinist, wrote poetry and painted, and was a first-class equestrienne.

After leaving St. Helena, Sylvain Lazarus (back row, top) spent time in Alaska. This picture was taken in 1902, on the ice shelf a mile from Nome.

Photo courtesy of the Western Jewish History Center, Judah L. Magnes Museum

Photo courtesy of the Western Jewish History Center, Judah L. Magnes Museum

L-R: Leontine Lazarus, Bernice Strauss and Sylvain Lazarus (age 4) in St. Helena. The Lazaruses adopted Bernice Strauss.

Felix Grauss, for many years the Postmaster of Calistoga, was arrested for his pro-German sentiments during World War I.

St. Helena Postmaster during World War I and again during World War II, Joe Galewsky was beloved by many but never wed.

NSGW parlor actually conducted Emanuel's funeral. When their mother Rebecca died in 1904, however, Rabbi Kaplin from San Francisco conducted the funeral at her home.

The local newspaper's paean to her revealed the esteem she held in town:

> Mrs. Galewsky's great characteristic was kindness of heart and we have never known any person more kindly disposed to all than she. It was always her pride and pleasure to be doing for others and many visitors to her home have felt the warmth of her hospitality and the gentleness of her ministrations. She was a kind, generous and good woman and the world is better for her having lived in it. [20]

Theodore Bell also enjoyed tremendous local esteem, but during the course of his career, he had made many enemies. One dark night in 1924, his car was run off the road on a lonely, dangerous pass in Bolinas. He died instantly, and there were many who suspected foul play. One local editor, John Walden of the *Napa Journal*, was so distraught that the day after Bell's untimely death there was no paper.

Whether or not Bell engaged in organized bootlegging is open to discussion. One man who definitely made a living in the business was Harry Brounstein, a liquor salesman whose territory included Minnesota, North Dakota and South Dakota, a part of the world where appetites for Canadian whiskey were big. Harry was quite successful before the Treasury Department caught up with him. Harry's son Al Brounstein grew up in Minneapolis, sledding in the winter and in the summer balancing on the handlebars of a borrowed bicycle. One day Al would recognize in the soils of the Napa Valley something that allowed him to make a very important contribution to the wine industry, and his opportunity to do so would be augmented by a little of the same daring his father possessed.[21]

The heirs of Harry Brounstein's employer would also have an

impact on the Napa Valley. Sam Bronfman, another Jew, bought the Bonaventura Liquor Store Company in Montreal in 1916 and sold liquor by mail order, which was legal during Canada's brief Prohibition period. When Prohibition ended in Canada, Sam and his brother started a distillery, and with the profits of that operation they were able to buy the much larger Joseph E. Seagram & Sons. The Bronfmans' endeavors accounted for a large portion of the booze smuggled into the US during the dry times.

The chasm that developed between urban Jews and rural Christians in the years around World War I was steeper than ever before in America. The Jews of the Napa Valley would certainly have felt this. Some had even run across a small but potent clause that appeared in real estate agreements. Land could only be sold, it said, to persons who were "white." Drawing from the anti-Asian prejudice of the Gold Rush days, this blanching of the populace was now being directed in Napa against African Americans, Mexicans, and Jews—the same groups targeted by the KKK, minus the Italians, who were beginning to hold positions of prominence in all the communities of the Napa Valley.

The failing economy, the presence of the Klan, increased violence, and a general narrowing of the public mind that began with the assault on Freedom of Speech and played out as Prohibition all combined to make the Napa Valley less inviting to Jews. Most of the Jewish shopkeepers whose ads had livened the newspapers with their price wars moved away, taking their "dry and fancy goods" with them. A few, like the Levinsons and Schwar(t)zes, Goodmans and Joe Galewsky, remained.

The price of land dropped. Bargains were to be had all over the Napa Valley for the investor with patient money. Solomon Gordon, known to all as "Sam," had a bit of this. Sam had made some money in San Francisco in the nickelodeon business. Nickelodeons, aka orchestrions, were coin-operated machines that played rolls of music, with pianos and other musical instruments built in. They were very popular in saloons before Prohibition and in speakeasies and cafes after 1920.

In 1921, he bought the old Napa Theatre, an elaborately designed entertainment house on First Street between Randolph and Franklin. He refurbished it, and in 1925 it re-emerged as the "Gordon Building," housing a number of small businesses. Although he was a rather quiet man, he liked to stand in front of his building, natty in his sportcoat, and greet passers-by. In a time of scarcity, Sam's success was a small beacon of hope for others.[22]

Neither tight money nor the KKK could scare off plucky Al (Kufflevitch) Kaufman, the Vallejo used furniture dealer. The Liberty Bonds he and everyone else had bought during the Great War started coming due during the early 1920s, and he invested his "warbucks" in the stock market, along with most of the proceeds of his business.

At first the Kaufmans' investments did so well that Al and Doris were able to indulge the many interests of their gifted daughter, Rozaline. They bought her a violin and private instruction, and she won a bronze medal and an invitation to play in a special orchestra composed of students from all over the state. She also took singing and dancing lessons. Making her own costumes, she went on tour as a performer with Olive de Leon's "Million Dollar Kitties," dancing and taking the stage as a soprano. She excelled in her academic studies at school and won admission to the College of the Pacific in Stockton.[23]

In the spring of 1929, however, the stock market's bubble burst. Like thousands of others, Rozaline had to abandon her studies and find work, which she did at Hale Brother's furniture store in San Francisco.

Facing bankruptcy, Al was forced to find a way to supplement his income. He turned not toward the city, but in the opposite direction. He scraped together as much money as he could and rented land in ultra-rural Pope Valley (in the northeast part of Napa

County), where he donned a cowboy hat and ran cattle for other ranchers. Little by little, he started coming out ahead.

Al wasn't the only Jewish cowboy in Pope Valley: Joe Yudnich, a fellow Pole, still had a large spread in the area. The gregarious ex-bootlegger hosted an annual 4th of July rodeo and cattle-branding party to which the new cowboy was invited. It was through this connection that Al Kaufman discovered twenty-two acres of land for sale at a good price in Pope Valley. Rich in grassy pastures, it was an ideal place to fatten livestock for the market. The Kaufmans bought it. They ran cattle and pigs and kept horses, and what used to be a furniture truck soon doubled as a livestock conveyer.

About the same time, another broke Jew was heading west. Sam Bickoff, a Ukrainian-born building contractor with nothing to build, packed his family into a Dodge with running boards and started across the country with his Russian-born wife Gussie, and their children Mel and Ellie, both "500% American." Ellie watched the Burma Shave signs fly by and kept a journal. The family slept in motor courts at night, paying 50¢ for a single room that housed all of them.[24]

When they arrived in Oakland, Sam started work as a door-to-door salesman, selling moth repellant on cardboard that could be hung in the closet. Soon he had a staff of salesmen to whom he supplied bobby pins, pencils, vanilla extract, chocolate pudding, and baking powder, all to be peddled door-to-door.

Russian Jews were finding their way to California, and a few, like Ellie Bickoff (who would one day be Ellie Meyer) would discover the Napa Valley. In the 1930s, however, the wine county had little to offer Jews who sought a life in the company of other Jews.

Chapter Eight

By the waters of Babylon we lay down and wept...
                                        —Psalm 137:1

BECAUSE OF PROHIBITION, NAPA COUNTY ACTUALLY ENTERED
America's Great Depression early. Wineries sold sacramental wine,
diversified, bootlegged or succumbed. Grape growers enjoyed a
boom that lasted for several years, because home winemaking for
personal use was still legal and because illegal producers in the
midwest bought grapes by the trainload. The bottom dropped out of
the grape industry in 1928, however. Farmers tore out their vines
and replanted with prunes and walnuts. When Repeal came in 1933,
not even bootlegging was profitable.

Only a handful of wineries remained, and after a decade of dis-
use, poor equipment yielded a mediocre product. Only on the cusp
of acceptance as an alternative to French wine when Prohibition
first came, the California wine industry now received barely a
glance from connoisseurs.

Nevertheless, a partnership of Jewish entrepreneurs hoped to
cash in on the Napa Valley's identity as a liquor source by estab-
lishing a plant to make brandy. They called it the Metropolitan Fruit

Distillery and their product "Mount Helena" brandy, and they employed twenty-five workers.[25] The principals were Sam Finkelstein (no relation to the Art Finkelstein family, who would arrive in the area in the 1970s), Philip Levin, and Abraham Schorr, a Czechoslovakian rabbi whose family had been in the liquor business in the old country. Schorr wanted to run the business under strict kosher rules, which meant that all the equipment had to be pristine and ritually cleaned with hot water prior to use and that only Sabbath-observing personnel could handle the ingredients and equipment. No non-kosher ingredients could be used in the process. A *mashgiach*[26] (perhaps Schorr himself) had to oversee the production, and everything needed to be sealed in his absence.

The idea might have taken off; Napa Valley bootleggers had made brandy by the barrelful and sold it to a steady stream of tourists throughout Prohibition. But Rabbi Schorr did not get along well with the Finkelsteins. He spent well beyond what the budget would allow, and when Finkelstein's wife and niece confronted Schorr about his excesses, he struck them both. They retaliated by snipping off the Orthodox rabbi's beard with a scissors and charging him with assault. His lawyer got him off, but the distillery folded, and in the long run the incident did not reflect well upon the Jewish community.[27]

The Jews in Petaluma were also raising eyebrows. A Communist cell was in the egg and poultry business there. (Some in the group were more politically minded than others.) One in particular liked to get up very early in the morning and distribute propaganda for the Communist Party. He left pamphlets on trees, telephone poles, and, in 1935, in a voting booth in Rutherford, a small community north of Yountville and south of St. Helena. *Strike!* the pamphlet urged. *If your wages are less than 40¢ an hour, strike!*

Most Napa Valley farm workers made between 25¢ and 30¢ an hour, but they wanted nothing to do with the Jewish chicken ranchers or their ideals.

Napa Valley officials passed a law banning the Communist

Party within county lines and organized a "vigilance committee" to eradicate it if it appeared. Jack Steckter, the local sheriff for two decades, had no qualms about violating the First Amendment. "Only by the adopting of prompt and stringent measures can an orderly season be enjoyed," said the *Napa Journal* in describing the danger that Steckter perceived from "Reds" in Sonoma County.[28] The cigar-chomping Steckter was fond of white Stetsons and the occasional bribe, and before he was thrown out of office for corruption in 1944, he ruled the Sheriff's Department with an iron hand. Thus there were no Reds in Napa County during the Depression and precious few Jewish liberals.

As the Depression deepened, poverty became a serious threat for many. There were quite a few suicides, but there were also helping hands for those healthy enough to work. The Sawyer Tannery continued to provide jobs for both men and women in its production of fleece-lined coats and baseball gloves. Mare Island, the largest industrial plant in Northern California, employed some 300 workers from Napa County and was responsible for the creation of other businesses, like the Basalt Corporation. These employers were important mainstays in the county's faltering economy, but on their own they were not sufficient to keep householders in the black.

Most American Jews in the 1930s had parents or grandparents who had been poor (or had been poor themselves). Identifying poverty as a collective and social rather than an individual and moral problem, most Jews had built into their lives a program of charitable giving to provide aid to those in distress. Jewish groups like B'nai B'rith and other philanthropies already had long histories in America. Hebrew Aid societies, refugee relief committees and other Jewish organizations gathered and distributed money and other forms of assistance both nationally and around the world. Jews were also major benefactors to non-Jewish charities. *Gemilut chasidim* (loving-kindness to others), a core Jewish value, was an element in the networking in which Jews had engaged for millennia.

The social measures Franklin Roosevelt took to ease the economic woes of the Great Depression felt invasive to many Protestants (especially in the upper classes) but were welcomed by most Jews, especially the Jewish leadership. They showed their appreciation by contributing generously to Roosevelt's Democratic Party, a trend that continues to the present day. (In time, however, many Jews would come to reconsider their regard for FDR.)

While Americans were adjusting to FDR's social programs, anti-Semitism continued to rise. Some individuals with great public esteem were outspoken in their prejudice. Automobile maker Henry Ford was one. He gave publicity to a crazed work called *Protocols of the Elders of Zion*, which purported to be minutes of a secret Jewish society. Failing to identify the Jewish tradition of networking as the natural and survival-oriented result of having family and business contacts scattered throughout the world, this paranoid bit of libel was dragged out as "proof" that the Jews were readying to take over the world. (Actually, *Protocols* was a pro-Czarist adaptation of an anti-Bonaparte document reformulated to discredit the Jews.) Ford's weekly newspaper, the *Dearborn Independent*, was a fountain of anti-Semitic hatred that kept on spouting until he was sued into apologizing.

Charles Lindbergh was another outspoken anti-Semite. The kidnapping of the aviation hero's daughter in 1932 spurred renewed public interest in everything about Lindbergh, including his fascistic political beliefs.

The Anglophilic president of at least one Ivy League college (Harvard) was also openly anti-Semitic.[29] Most of these schools now imposed quotas on the numbers of Jews they would admit into their graduate and undergraduate programs. Harvey Posert Sr., the father of a future St. Helenan, was among the few Jews admitted to Yale under the quota system. It was still in existence in 1952, when Harvey Jr. graduated from the same institution.

In the midst of this increase in publicly proclaimed hate, it was an ethnic Jew whose arrival in Napa spelled salvation for many who would otherwise not have found work. Nearly penniless and unable to speak English when he arrived in San Francisco in 1906, Nathan Rothman peddled, swept floors and worked as a porter and a shipping clerk until he finally landed a job as a salesman for a clothing firm.[30] In this capacity he was able to travel throughout the western states, creating a network that would one day become very useful to him.

By 1919 he had accumulated $500, enough to start a small company manufacturing men's pants. "NR" and his wife Ray did all the work by themselves at first in a small loft in San Francisco. Their product caught on, and in 1925 they moved to a bigger plant on Howard Street, where they employed 125 workers. As the business continued to grow they introduced a new line, woolen slacks, and opened a subsidiary plant on Fremont Street. In 1932 they renamed their venture "Rough Rider." By the mid 1930s, Rough Rider was doing quite well.

Desperate for a mid-sized manufacturing concern to come to Napa and breathe some life into the place, city officials wooed Rothman. Napa merchant Bert Voorhees and Cap Garner, head of the struggling Chamber of Commerce, spearheaded a "Move Rough Rider to Napa" campaign. To sweeten the pot, the city council promised that if Rough Rider employed 300 people, the land upon which the plant was built would revert to Rothman. Toward this end, local citizens raised $25,000 by public subscription to buy acreage on Soscol Avenue. The plan succeeded, and in 1936 Rothman, his pants-making equipment and his key employees set up operations in a building on Soscol Avenue, on the banks of the Napa River.

Rothman had assured Napans that his business could employ as many as 500 people, with a payroll of $240,000.[31] The reality far outdistanced his predictions; at one time some 900 people drew paychecks from the company that became the largest employer in the city of Napa. Rothman added another facility on Oak Street in Napa and a ladies' apparel division in Vallejo. The Rothmans lived in Hillsborough, but NR was chauffeured to the Napa facility every day.

A very important Napa gentile who got his start at Rough Rider was George Altamura.[32] NR overheard George, age eighteen, pleading with NR's brother Harry for work one morning and said, "What kind of business are we, if we can't hire a young man who wants to work?" George got a job carrying bundles of clothes for $35 a week—just enough to keep body and soul together. He worked all the way up the ladder to be a finished presser, which gave him the experience he needed to start his own dry cleaning enterprise several years later. George was able to parlay the money he made in his dry cleaning business into holdings of land in Napa and the Valley at large. One of the properties he bought was the Gordon Building. Sam Gordon was one of Altamura's role models, along with Nat Rothman.

Jewish advocates had urged the relocation of Jewish-run industries from urban centers to outlying areas since the days of Baron de Hirsch. Densely populated clusters of urban Jews, while creating an environment that reinforced age-old Jewish traditions, also threatened to replicate the European ghetto experience. Release from poverty and the prejudice that it attracted could be assisted, many hoped, through population dispersal, if not to desolate farming locations, then to rural communities in need of small businesses.[33]

The coming of Rough Rider to Napa was thoroughly in the spirit of this philosophy. A "magnet effect" also occurred: once some Jews chose Napa as a place to live, others followed. Many of the men whom Rothman hired to run his departments moved to the Napa Valley. Invested with strong leadership qualities, several Rough Rider executives became cornerstones of the Jewish community that would eventually gather in Napa (although NR himself converted to Christianity). Among these were Ilya ("Chick") and George Gordon, Dan Weinstein, Sam Weinstock, Boyd Margolis, Abe Casper and Nat Rothman's brother Harry. Rothman's nephew Donald Broverman also became a Rough Rider executive with a Napa address. Don's brother Daniel Broverman bought Napa's dilapidated Palace Hotel from the Bank of America and tried to restore it, a task that proved impossible.[34]

Another nephew, Julian Weidler, started working for Rough Rider in 1932, while he was still a student at Berkeley. Julian's parents, William and Rebecca Feldman Weidler, were both immigrants, he from Austria-Hungary, she and her five sisters from Romania. They met in San Francisco before the great earthquake and fire, where William worked for a while as a maitre d' at the posh Palace Hotel there. He went into business buying merchandise at auction and then selling the second-hand goods.

Son Julian started as a clerk in Nathan Rothman's shipping room and eventually became president of the company, a position he held for almost twenty years. Julian Weidler's contributions to the community did not end with his business life. He served the people of Napa County in a number of leadership positions throughout the next seven decades.

* * *

The same economic crisis that crippled America in the 1930s and early '40s also seized the countries of Europe. Europeans who were poor before these dark years became poorer still. In Cluj Napoka/Koloszvar, the little Hungarian/Romanian city that Zoltan Rosenberger had fled before becoming a peddler in Mexico, the students at the local university had taken to beating up Jews and breaking the windows of their houses. Sara Simon, the youngest daughter of a Jewish tailor and his book-peddling wife, watched these occurrences with alarm, especially when some of the students took to wearing armbands with swastikas.

Sara's older sister applied for a travel visa. Unable to go to America because of the quota system, she chose Mexico as her destination, but the visa would only be good for six months. Their oldest sister Rose had already gone to Mexico, married a man named Martin Elefant, and established a shoe store in Juarez. By the time the visa arrived many weeks later, the second sister had fallen in love and decided not to go. Sara went in her place, a decision that proved auspicious for many reasons.

Far from being intimidated by the scope of this immense solo journey, Sara discovered that she had a strong sense of adventure. Her itinerary took her first to New York, where she stayed briefly with relatives, and then by train through Texas to the Mexican border. Along the way she found herself being "adopted" by young women around her own age who taught her rudimentary English. The new world, she decided, was far more delightful and welcoming than the old one she had left behind.

Sara soon discovered that a skinny, sad-looking fellow was clerking and sleeping in the back room of the Elefants' store. He had been a mattress hauler and before that a peddler. He was a Hungarian Jew, indeed from her own hometown, but he was penniless and stricken with exceedingly bad luck. He seemed to have lost whatever spirit of adventure had sent him from his native land. At first she hardly gave Zoltan Rosenberger a second look.

By now Sara had no intention of returning to Europe. Her brother-in-law wanted to arrange a convenient marriage for her with a wealthy older man from another city so she could avoid deportation, but as the weeks went by, the emaciated store clerk started to perk up, perhaps because there was an intelligent Jewish girl in his presence. Sara, in turn, observed that Zoltan was honest and sincere, and there was no doubt about his willingness to work hard.

The fact that Sara Simon was in need of a husband was the first piece of good fortune that had fallen Zoltan's way since he'd left Cluj. He decided to press his luck. He asked her to marry him.

Incredibly, she accepted. They wed in 1936, and to take advantage of the fact that there was a new member who might add to the family's coffers, the Elefants built another, larger store in a nearby town. Exultant, Zoltan headed off for his new store to receive his first shipment of shoes—which through no fault of his own fell off a collapsing bridge, dropped into a river and floated away. Bad luck hadn't entirely disappeared, but things were looking up.

Among the most severely compromised countries in Europe was Germany, which had to pay enormous reparations for the harm it had caused in the Great War. Spiraling inflation and political chaos inaugurated *angst*, and as always, many sought targets upon whom to vent their emotions. No politician was more adept at focusing the hiss and poison of German anxiety than the frustrated artist, Adolph Hitler. Hitler had slithered up Germany's political ranks and into the hearts of his countrymen with a doctrine of intense anti-Semitism. Even before he became Chancellor in 1933, Hitler's supporters initiated attacks against Jews.[35]

For the stolid citizens of the hamlet of Barntrup near Hanover, for example, the Nazi Party was practically a religion in itself. Young Egon Katz was forced to salute the Fuehrer with the rest of his classmates at the beginning of each school day.[36] The only Jew in the school, Egon endured a steady pounding of anti-Semitic jokes and diatribes that finally led to his dropping out. In 1933, when he was seventeen, he apprenticed with a Jewish baker in Saarland, part of the autonomous area known as the Rheinland, which was virtually 100% Catholic but thought to be more hospitable to Jews. Hitler quickly gobbled up the region, and the Jewish baker under whom Egon was working fled to Lorraine, France. Egon stayed to finish his training.

With his Rheinlander address and his Hanoverian (non-Yiddish) accent, many were unaware that Egon was Jewish. Indeed, so thorough was his ability to fool the local Gestapo that he was drafted into the German army.

"*Herr Leutnant,*" he told the draft board lieutenant, while standing stiffly at attention, "*ich bin ein Jude.*" "Lieutenant, Sir, I'm a Jew."

"*Ruhn! Austreten!*" barked the Lieutenant: "At ease! Dismissed!" If he had been only half Jewish, Egon would have been drafted; if the incident had occurred a year or two later, he could have been arrested (or worse). As it turned out, he was simply released to return to work.

Now that the truth was known, however, prudence dictated another change of residence. He moved to Berlin, where he found work for a baker who was, as it turned out, a prominent Nazi. The man took a liking to the new assistant and encouraged him to join the *Sturmabteilung*, the elite Storm Troopers also known as the SS. Horrified and repelled, Egon slipped away to Hamburg, where, at least for a while, he was able to conceal his origins. His brother Bruno was also there. Bruno had certain connections, which would prove surprisingly helpful.

In 1935 the Nazi government passed the "Nuremberg Laws," which deprived Jews of their citizenship and stripped them of their right to do such mundane things as fraternize with gentiles and operate motor vehicles. Other, increasingly harsh persecutions followed, including a rule requiring Jews to wear a yellow, star-shaped patch, as they had been forced to do during medieval times.

A devastating turn for the worse came in November, 1938, in an orgy of hate and destruction remembered as "Kristallnacht," when everything identifiably Jewish in Germany was smashed, burned and obliterated. The next morning, when the survivors sifted through the rubble, they discovered that 500 synagogues had been torched, 7,000 businesses destroyed, 30,000 Jews had been arrested and 90 were dead.[37]

In the city of Barntrup, Jew-haters smashed the Katz's windows. The Nazis had forced an impoverished elderly man to move in with Egon's parents. On Kristallnacht a mob pushed the old man out of the house and onto the street and made him march with a sign hanging from his neck that read, "This is what a rich Jew looks like."

Elisabeth Rosenthal, a student nurse, watched in horror that November night as scores sought refuge in the Frankfurt hospital where she worked. Surgeons operated around the clock on healthy patients to conceal them from the SS soldiers who marched into the facility with their guns and black uniforms. Throughout the night she tried to telephone her parents in her hometown of Fuerth, but to no avail: They had disappeared, as she knew she herself must do if she were to survive. (She later learned that they had survived the night.)

As soon as she could, Elisabeth Rosenthal joined the 100,000-150,000 other Jews who were fleeing Germany during the months after Kristallnacht. Her destination was England. The exit fees were exorbitant, but Elisabeth could leave because her family had enjoyed wealth before Hitler's conquest of the German people, and a small amount of it remained.

This was not the first time the growing Nazi scourge had interrupted Elisabeth's education. When she was attending the public high school in Fuerth, two men in suits entered the classroom and arrested her German literature teacher, who was Jewish. She was never seen again.

As the schools in Fuerth fell ever more fully under the thrall of Nazi doctrine, Elisabeth (only half Jewish—her mother was a Lutheran) found herself increasingly drawn to Judaism. She convinced her parents to send her to an Orthodox private school. Later, when the Nazis ordered the school to close, the students were told to choose a career. Elisabeth chose nursing, a decision she might have regretted that horrible night in November 1938.

Egon Katz's facade had protected him so well that even after Kristallnacht he not only fraternized with gentiles, he dated Christian women (an offense punishable by death) and, for a living, drove a motorized delivery tricycle for the Nazi baker who employed him, also an illegal activity for a Jew. He might have continued the ruse indefinitely had he not had an accident with the delivery bike and gotten hauled before a Nazi judge. He was found guilty of causing the mishap and was released, but the next morning (when he was astride the bike again) the Gestapo stopped him and ordered him to report to the *Polizeiamt* early the next day. This time Egon ran for his life.

Unable to enter Holland, his first choice of refuge, he managed to escape to Denmark. Exhausted and spiritually drained, he sought guidance there from a Danish rabbi, who rather than consolation gave him a vicious dressing down. Then the Danish police appeared and whisked Egon back to Germany, where he was thrown into the notorious Slensburg prison. Several weeks later he was released, but the buzzards were circling. The increasingly predatory Nazis arrested his sisters and sent one to Ravensrueck and another to Theresienstadt, a concentration camp in Czechoslovakia. A third sister was shipped to Treblinka. All three died.

It was his brother Bruno who arrived at the eleventh hour with the gift of life for Egon. It came in the form of a boat ticket to Shanghai, where he joined some 17,000 other Jewish refugees. From there he would make his way to the United States, where he would meet Elisabeth Rosenthal, the nurse from Fuerth.

*   *   *

Another German Jew whose path would one day lead him to the Napa Valley was Leo Trepp.[38] He was born in Mainz. Touched by the city's deep, rich Jewish heritage, he knew he wanted to spend his life absorbing Judaica but was uncertain whether to approach it as a rabbi or a professor. Therefore he did both, earning his rabbinical degree and his PhD simultaneously at the University of Wurzburg. He was ordained in 1936.

He had two pulpits to choose between: a prestigious one in

Berlin and one in Oldenburg, a city in distress with the Nazis' rise to power. He selected the latter, and in 1938 he married Miriam de Haas, the daughter of his predecessor. At his father's urging he sought a larger pulpit and was hired to take over a synagogue in Cologne, a job that would begin in 1939.

Being a rabbi in Germany in the late 1930s was more than dangerous. Alert to the gathering peril, the Trepps began to suspect they might be wise to leave Germany before the new job began. The ominous "J" stamped on their passports, however, barred their exit through conventional routes. In the summer of 1938 Miriam contacted an acquaintance, the chief rabbi of the British Empire, asking his assistance in leaving the country. "You are the captain and must go down with the ship" was the reply.

On Kristallnacht, all the Jews in Oldenburg were dragged to the town barracks. The Nazis released the women the next morning but forced the men, including Leo Trepp, to march through the town and into the jail. Miriam Trepp sent a telegram to the chief rabbi of the British Empire: "The ship has sunk," it said.

Now there was no synagogue for Leo to work in. Their anxiety deepened. They knew the best hope for their survival was to somehow get to America, but the US refused to grant them visas. By 1940 they were finally able to procure passage to England, where they applied again for visas through the US Embassy in London. While they waited, prayed and hid from the Nazis' rocket attacks, they learned English and helped care for 200 children who had been transported there from Germany.

After a year, the US Consul told them that their visa applications had been denied because the guarantee (payment) offered on their behalf was not sufficient: they weren't wealthy enough to be saved. Miriam immediately wrote the two aunts in Rochester, NY who had agreed to sponsor them and told them of the dilemma. Original stockholders of the Eastman Kodak Company, the aunts pulled strings, and the visas arrived. The Trepps boarded a ship for America, and in time their journey for a safe haven would bring them to the Napa Valley.

*   *   *

Wealth and connections would prove to be, for many, the difference between life on foreign shores and death in Europe. A future St. Helenan who had both of these prerequisites was Hanns Kornblum, who would one day change his name to Hanns Kornell.[39]

The Kornblum family lived in Mainz, which was in the heart of the wine country. Like the Beringer family, a gentile Mainz lineage, the Kornblums had been in the wine business for three generations when Hitler began his ascent to power. Their Schoenberger Kabinett cellars were built over the remains of a medieval monastery that featured a tunnel under the Rhine River, where monks might make surreptitious visits to the nuns in the nearby cloister. The Kornblums' close friends included other European wine- and champagne-making families, like the Taittingers.

Hanns had attended Wolfenbittel, an exclusive preparatory school for wealthy Jewish boys, and then graduated with a degree in enology from Geisenheim University, the German equivalent of today's UC Davis. He was skiing in Bavaria during Kristallnacht, and when he heard what had happened he tried to cross into Switzerland, but the border patrol stopped him and turned him in to the SS. He was marched off to Dachau.

The SS gave Hanns' family in Mainz twenty-four hours to gather their things and leave. They hid in the trunk of their limousine and had their chauffeur drive them to France, but Nazi sympathizers there turned them in to the authorities. They were sent to concentration camps. Hanns' father died in Theresienstadt in Czechoslovakia; his mother and the others vanished, and the Third Reich snatched the material wealth of three generations of German Jewish Kornblums. It was a scene that repeated itself throughout Germany.

Hanns remained in Dachau for almost a year. In 1939, he was released.[40] He went to England and worked as a dishwasher and then in 1940 sailed to America, leaving behind any desire to practice Judaism.

The Fromm family had also been in the wine industry for multiple generations. Like Hanns Kornell, young Alfred Fromm graduated from Geisenheim. He joined the family business, "N. Fromm, Wine Growers and Shippers" in 1924 and became its export manager. His job brought him to America and the Napa Valley in 1933, just after Prohibition had come to an end. Alfred saw great potential in being on hand for the wine industry's rebirth, especially if Europe went to war and the supply of European wines was interrupted. He emigrated for good in 1936 and the following year joined a small wine brokerage in New York. He soon landed a deal to become the exclusive representative of an up-and-coming Napa Valley winery: Christian Brothers.

At first, many Americans mistook Alfred Fromm for a bootlegger-turned-legit, an identification that the young aristocrat found disturbing.[41] Even more disturbing, however, was the "offer" a Nazi official made in 1938 to his father, Max, to buy N. Fromm for a fraction of its value. The alternative was the concentration camp.[42] Aware of the grave danger facing the loved ones he had left in Germany, Alfred was able to finance the escape of thirty-seven family members to the safe shores of the United States.[43]

Before the war's end, a man who really had been a bootlegger—Sam Bronfman—reunited Alfred with an old friend from Germany, Franz Sichel. H. Sichel & Sohne was established in 1857 and produced a popular wine, Blue Nun. Alfred and Franz became Fromm & Sichel, importers and distributors. Their stunning success representing Christian Brothers helped to revitalize the Napa Valley's slumping alcoholic beverage industry and saved the Order's wine business from bankruptcy.

* * *

The Nazis began their bid for world domination in 1939. Poland, whose government had actually admired and supported Hitler, was the first target. Overwhelmed by a *blitzkrieg* of tanks and mortars, Poland's cities were destroyed and many of its people carted off and relocated. Its Jews were forced into labor and concentration camps or killed outright.[44]

In what seems like a strange contradiction, some Polish Jews were conscripted to fight in the war. Joseph Michalski was in the Polish Cavalry, a Jew conscripted to fight for the Germans.[45] The Russians captured him and interned him for a while in a POW camp in the Ukrainian city of Lvov, an event that actually saved his life. While he was there, he wrote to his nineteen-year-old girlfriend, Fela, asking her to come be with him; he could take care of her there. She and her brother left their family and headed for Russia in the deep of winter, thinking at the time that the camps to which the rest of her (and Joseph's) family were being taken would keep them safe throughout the rest of the war. They were wrong: Everyone in both families perished except Joseph, Fela and her brother.

Norway, Holland, Belgium and France all fell easily into Hitler's grasp, the task in those countries made easier by the anti-Semites there.

Adolph Hitler's plan was to kill every Jew in the world, starting with the ones closest at hand. Before Pearl Harbor, shiploads of fleeing families suspected something like this was afoot and tried to find port in the US. President Roosevelt turned them away and did nothing to promote their safe haven anywhere on earth. Likewise, Great Britain closed the doors of Palestine to Jewish refugees.

Roosevelt's excuse was that he feared stimulating American anti-Semitism by promoting a further influx of impoverished Jews. Such a move, his wife once explained, could endanger his bid for re-election.[46] A somewhat less callous explanation was that FDR wanted Congress to agree to America's participation in the war in

Europe and feared a backlash against the idea, should he seem too friendly toward the Jews. Anti-Semitism continued in America as the country battled with the Great Depression.

Recent Roosevelt apologists have pointed out that few were truly aware of the extent of Hitler's insanity.[47] Jews had been mistreated in Europe for nearly 2,000 years, and the cruelty they were receiving under Hitler at first seemed like merely more of the same. Finally in 1944 Secretary of the Treasury Henry Morganthau, a Jew, convinced FDR that America needed to respond pro-actively to their plight.

Existing refugee relief groups cranked into higher gear, and other committees were formed to raise money and increase public awareness. Wily Egon Katz and the nurse Elisabeth Rosenthal were both recipients of this charity. They discovered each other at the Jewish Community Center in San Francisco, after Egon had Americanized his name to "Gene." They would one day marry and eventually buy a home in Napa.

The ones in most urgent need of relief, however, were not the refugees, but those unable to flee.

Karola Bien was among these. Karola lived in a Polish ghetto with her parents and sister, and when she realized that the Germans were coming to haul off the Jewish population, she hid in the attic of the place where she worked. The Nazis arrested her family and forced them into a labor camp not far from the city.[48]

For four weeks, Karola huddled among the rafters, peering cautiously out the window from time to time. From her vantage point above the shop, she could watch her mother and father come to the city each morning, en route to the place where they were made to work. One morning she saw that her father was alone. Later she learned that all the women had been detained in the camp that day, and while the men were gone they were murdered.

The shop manager who risked his life to shelter Karola also procured false papers for her so that she could escape to Warsaw. In

1940 the ghetto there had contained some 500,000 Jews, but by 1942 only some 40,000 remained, the rest having been, in the Nazis' words, "liquidated."[49]

Karola's brother had changed his name and joined the underground resistance, which had connections outside the ghetto that included the shopkeeper who had hidden Karola. The brother found her a housekeeping job in a home whose original Polish occupants had been carted off. The family, high-ranking Nazis from Berlin, also employed two other Jews as household staff, and when they moved away to press the war elsewhere they put an ad in the local newspaper recommending the services of their three employees.

Karola realized that in providing creature comforts for the Nazis, she could secure her survival. She accepted a job with another German family after the departure of the first and was in Warsaw in 1943 to witness the uprising of the underground and the reprisals that followed as the Nazis razed the ghetto, building by building. When the second German family departed, they gave Karola a year's salary in advance, believing that they would be returning with the spoils of battle after the war was won. They never came back.

With Warsaw in ruins, Karola fled to Cracow, where a family of peasants took her in. In time, she was able to go to America and become part of the thriving Jewish community in New York City, which had been a haven for Jewish refuges since its infancy, starting with the Sephardim escaping Recife. Her final years would bring her to the Napa Valley.

An ocean away, the America of the late 1940s offered the same respite from oppression that it had a century earlier. It was one of the few places on the war-torn planet where Jews could heal and start anew...

Chapter Nine

In that day each of you will invite his neighbor
to sit under his vine and fig tree, declares the Lord
Almighty.   *—Zechariah 3:10*

FRED AND BELLA ROSENTHAL—NO RELATION TO THE NURSE
Elisabeth Rosenthal Katz—managed to slip out of Germany with
their ten-year-old daughter, Lottie, before Lottie was able to
process the meaning of star-shaped patches and broken glass. Fred
had been a textile salesman before Kristallnacht and somehow
made his way to America.[50]

It was the hope of Lottie's parents that their daughter would
never have to face the cruel reality of anti-Semitic prejudice. They
sought a quiet place in the country, as far from the slingers of hate
and breakers of windows as they could go while remaining within
traveling distance of a major city. The sleepy Napa Valley fit the
bill. They bought land on West Salvador Avenue (now Wine
Country Avenue) in Napa with a cousin, John Marx, and went into
the egg business.[51]

At first, Bella tried to maintain a kosher table, which meant
that meat had to be brought in from San Francisco by Greyhound
bus. After a few instances when the meat spoiled because the bus

company failed to say that it had arrived, Bella gave up. Orthodoxy, it seemed, was a luxury that farm folk had to abandon, especially with no synagogue within walking distance.

Aside from the Jews at Rough Rider and a few old families, there were very few practicing Jews in Napa and even fewer up-valley. The Rosenthals and John Marx attended services in Vallejo with other Napans, notably the families of Joe Lazarus (who owned an auto supply store in the Major Building, next to the old Opera House), the Charlups (furniture dealers) and the Baylinsons. Often, instead of shlepping to Solano County, the families would meet at the Baylinsons', who had the largest house, or at Joe Lazarus' auto supply store. Sometimes they would worship with Al and Doris (Kufflevitch) Kaufman and their daughter Rozaline, who by 1940 was working for Sears, Roebuck in Napa and spending her weekends horseback riding on the Pope Valley ranch. The Levys and the Israelskys might also be there, as would some of the executives from Rough Rider. Lazarus was the president of the small Jewish congregation. On High Holy Days most of them went to one of the temples in San Francisco.

Other Napa Jews, however, had become more or less assimilated. The Manasses, for example, did not identify much with the rest of the Jewish community.

Although they were not religious, contractor/ mothball salesman Sam Bickoff wanted his daughter Ellie to socialize with other Jewish teenagers, something she was not doing in Oakland. He moved the family to Los Angeles, but the children longed for their old Northern California stomping grounds. After graduation, Ellie and her big brother Mel attended Berkeley, sharing an apartment.

It was at Berkeley that Ellie finally found other Jewish students whom she could enjoy. During a Jewish mixer at the International House there, she met one in particular: a young man from Vallejo named Wesley Meyer, whose parents had a jewelry store. Ellie was a good dancer, and Wes kept asking her to dance. Before she could accept, however, she had to ask her brother's permission, and when Wes invited her to go for ice cream with him and his friends after the event, Mel at first refused. It took some convincing (Wes reminded Mel that Mel already knew some of the other students in the group) before he finally acquiesced.

It was the first of many dates. They decided to "go steady," and one Sunday Ellie made *latkes* for her beau. Wes told his mother that he had met a girl who made *latkes* better than she did. Lena immediately telephoned Ellie and invited her to Vallejo for the weekend. With Mel's approval, she went.

They got engaged, and when Wesley graduated they married. He was twenty-one, and she was eighteen.

Papa Isadore Meyer wanted to see that his son had a good start. He told him of a jewelry store in Napa that was going through bankruptcy court (like all too many businesses in the Napa Valley at that time). Was he interested? He could buy it and give it to Wes to manage for a monthly salary of $85. Wes demurred, for in the meantime headhunters had contacted him and offered him the same salary with promises of quick promotions. Isadore came back with a counter offer of $100 per month and the option for Ellie to work in the store for $12.50 a week. Each having negotiated the deal to his own satisfaction, the son entered the father's profession. The original Meyers Jewelers in Napa was on First Street between Main and Brown.

It was a nice life, far from the troubles that the newspapers were reporting in Europe. Yet even in the bucolic Napa Valley were traces of the same hate that had grown so lethal to so many. Understated, it was a quiet, sneaky kind of hate, present in the language of real estate documents written to exclude "non-whites" from owning or occupying homes in certain parts of town; revealed openly not to adults but sometimes to children. Claire Levy, niece of pioneers Joe and Charlie Levinson, felt it often from Germans on their way to the church near her home. "*Schwarze*," they called her: "Blackie." It was meant to be insulting, and it stung. Her brother

Harold, the only Jewish boy in his class at Napa High School, heard it daily from other teens.

When Japan bombed Pearl Harbor in December of 1941 and the United States entered World War II, Harold Levy immediately quit school and joined the Navy, not for reasons of patriotic devotion, but to get out of Napa and his role as class scapegoat. He was assigned to the tanker *Neosho*, a huge supply ship sent to tend the Navy in the Coral Sea. Early in 1942 the *Neosho* was destroyed when a Japanese plane fell or crashed into it. Harold was listed as missing, and finally as dead. He was seventeen.

Just a few years older, Wesley and Ellie Meyer knew of Harold's tragic fate. By the time America entered World War II, they had two children, a boy and a girl. The Meyers had leased a new store to house their growing jewelry business and had just finished refurbishing it the day before Wes received orders to report for active duty. Having been in ROTC at Berkeley, he entered the Army Air Corps as a second lieutenant. He served for a time as an investigative officer in the States before sailing to North Africa as a troop commander.

Lt. Meyer's first assignment was with the 20th Air Depot Group, where he helped to service, maintain and supply the US planes flying over Italy and Southern France. His prior investigative work then led him to become a combat photographer with the Office of Strategic Services (OSS, the forerunner of the Central Intelligence Agency): spy work.

One of his informants was an Italian cleric in Rome, known to him only by a contact number. Wes described meeting his counterpart to *Napa County Recorder* columnist Nancy Brennan:

> After the Germans were pushed out of Rome, I took
> a jeep and went up to meet him. I was very surprised
> to find that his name was Luigi Guinta of the Vatican,
> and that he was in charge of all the Masses that Pope
> Pius XII held. Then I understood why he was able to

give me such good information, because he was in
contact with all the churches, little and large, in all
of Italy. And he had his priests and all their parishioners
on the look out (sic) for any information that would be of
value to us. We always had our "drops" contact the
local priests, wherever they could.[52]

Guinta told Wes that he had hidden twelve Jewish children in
the Vatican. Wes appealed among his men on their behalf for clothing, blankets and C-rations.

After the war, Guinta arranged for Wes to meet with the Pope
in a private audience that included a dozen devout Catholics.

I watched everybody make the sign of the cross, and
kiss the Ring of the Fisherman, and I tried to do the
same...but the Pope looked at me and said, "My
son, you're not Catholic, are you." [I] responded,
"No, I'm not. I'm Jewish, but how did you know?"
"That's my little secret," said the Pope.[53]

While the gregarious Wesley Meyer performed humanitarian
acts in Europe, a few Jewish Napans engaged in good works at
home. Sam Grossman was appointed to the Advisory Board of
Napa State Hospital. His brother Harry served on the Grand Jury
that brought to an end the career of a local tyrant, strong-arm sheriff Jack Steckter. As owner of Albert's department store, Harry
Grossman may have been one of the few people in Napa who did-
n't fear the powerful man in the white Stetson.[54]

Other Napa County Jews, however, laid low and tried not to
"make waves." Japanese families were being hauled off to intern-
ment camps throughout the West Coast, and the Jews in
Europe...there were rumors. Some feared the same fate could be
waiting for them. "Don't make waves" became a shibboleth for the
tiny Jewish population in Napa County. The group that had been
meeting together for Shabbat services quietly drifted apart.

The war ended.

                                    *   *   *

    Having survived the Nazis from behind the borders of Russia,
Joseph and Fela Michalski started a family. So many Russian men
had died in the war that Stalin gave incentives of food and other
goods to families who had children. When their second child,
Henry, was born, women in their small village offered to trade him
for jewels and other valuables. They declined. Unwilling to remain
in a Communist country amidst potential baby-thieves, the
Michalskis walked to Bavaria, where they lived for three years in a
Displaced Persons' Camp. They hoped to immigrate to Palestine.
Zionist groups there were smuggling in Jews. Fela's brother and his
new little family eventually settled in Tel Aviv, and the Michalskis
were ready to join them, their boxes already stamped with
"Michalski Family Tel Aviv," when President Truman announced
that he had expanded the American quota to let in 120,000 more
refugees. "We're going to America!" cried Joseph.

    Rozaline Kaufman was all grown up by the time the war
ended. Roz spent her weekends in Pope Valley on the family ranch,
where she and her steed, "Lady West Wind," had become familiar
sights at local parades. Horses and horsemanship were all the rage
in the Napa Valley during World War II and the years that followed
it. Like her friends and co-religionists the Charlups, she belonged
to the local Horseman's Association. She worked at Sears, Roebuck
and lived for her days off.
    Land in the Napa Valley was cheap, and like her parents Al and
Doris, Roz had a yen to own a spread of her own. When forty-three
acres of rocky, rolling countryside became available near the
Silverado Trail in the tiny hamlet of Oakville, she bought it with a
down-payment of $10, employing as a witness to the mortgage-
signing a neighbor who happened to be a German prisoner-of-war-

just released from the POW camp up the road in Rutherford. As egalitarian as she had been when she was sewing gauze masks for the ladies of the night in Vallejo, Rozaline did not hold grudges.

In 1950 her horsemanship took her to Hawaii, where she marched in a big parade with members of other riding associations. Among the riders was an Army officer named Bert Johnson. Roz and Bert hit it off, and after a whirlwind courtship they rode off into the sunset together. Although he was an Episcopalian, Roz convinced Bert to attend Jewish services with her, and the two were husband and wife for the next fifty years. Al and Doris, meanwhile, passed on to whatever rest or adventures awaited them.

*   *   *

Down in Mexico, the Rosenbergers had opened a shoe store of their own in Baja California. This time Zoltan and Sara's shipments of wares did not fall into the river, no revolutions forced the closure of their store, and people actually paid their bills. Sometimes the shop sold out nearly completely, and they were forced to stock the shelves with empty boxes so that it seemed like they still had something to sell. They made enough money to pay off their debts and start accumulating savings.

Now that they were Mexican citizens, the restrictive immigration laws that had barred their entrance to America no longer applied. They could, if they so chose, uproot themselves and their growing family and sample life north of the border.

They so chose; but ever so cautiously. The Elefants (Sara's sister and brother-in-law) had opened a furniture store in Brawley, California. Zoltan entered into partnership with them and came to America, while Sara remained with the children in Baja. For three years they lived with a foot in both countries, unwilling to sacrifice the stable and steady source of income they had established on their own. Zoltan's prudence—a trait learned the hard way—paid off. The Elefants started making decisions with which he could not agree, so Zoltan returned to Mexico, glad to have Sara and a safe business to come home to.

America, however, was worth a second look. They would try again soon.

*   *   *

Wesley Meyer came back from the war in February 1946. "Prepare for invasion," he wired his wife. "Coming home immediately. P.S. I love you. Wesley Meyer."[55] The former OSS officer did prepare an assault: on the jewelry business. Rewarded for his heroism with a full partnership by his father, Wes rolled up his sleeves and prepared to turn Meyers Jewelers into a major money-making enterprise. Instead of tanks, bucks started rolling in.

Also rolling in, slowly at first, were stories about the Holocaust, the fiery and absolute destruction that had befallen the Jews of Europe under the torch of the Third Reich. It was hard for most to comprehend, at first, that 6,000,000 people had perished. (Five and-a-half million, for example, was the total number of Jews alive in the United States at the turn of the 21st century.) American Jewry taxed itself to come up with $100,000,000 to help its cousins overseas in 1946. In 1948 it gathered $250,000,000.[56]

Julian Weidler, by now President of Rough Rider, led the ingathering effort in Napa through the Jewish Welfare Fund. In addition to raising money to help refugees abroad, he also spearheaded charitable assistance for Jews leaving urban ghettos for work in Northern California. The money went to help with gas and food expenses. In 1947 he organized Napa's first B'nai B'rith chapter and became its president.[57]

The common wisdom of the time among most Jews, however, was to look forward not back: to forget the sealed boxcars, poison gas, missing family members.[58] It was a practice many Napa Jews worked to perfect.

Public sentiment towards the Jews took on something of a multiple personality in the late 1940s. Universities still had quotas; country clubs and even neighborhoods still excluded. On the other hand, Congress passed a resolution urging President Truman to work toward opening Palestine as a new Zion, a homeland, for the Diaspora.

Britain, however, did not want to release its control of Palestine. It resisted until rowdy public demonstrations made it difficult for it to continue its pro-Arab policy, at which time it turned the knotty matter back to the United Nations to unravel. On November 29, 1947 the UN voted to rescind British control and divide the region into Arab and Jewish provinces. The Arabs were enraged.

On May 14, 1948 Israel became a real, bona fide country once again, after 2,000 years. Future Napan Donna Dover, who would one day be Donna Mendelsohn, remembered the day:

> My parents, siblings and I were living at my grandparents' house
> in Rock Island, Illinois while our house was being remodeled
> (my mother was expecting twins). The vote and proceedings
> were being broadcast on the radio and my family was glued
> to it when it was announced that Israel had declared itself a
> State and that Harry Truman said that the US was the first
> nation to recognize it. There was pandemonium in the room.
> I remember my grandmother baking up a storm of strudel
> and *mandelbrot* (she called it *kumish brot*) to bring to a
> party, and she made these huge pots of coffee (in those days
> they only had percolators on the gas stove) at the Farband
> Hall. Everyone was very excited.

The following day, however, five Arab countries attacked the infant nation. Although outmanned and outgunned, the Israelis held them off. The troubled region might have drawn the rest of the world into their conflict, but the superpowers' attentions turned to other, equally knotty problems in North Korea.

The Jews of Napa, sequestered from world affairs and without a leader, made no public demonstration of joy over the creation of Israel. A few, like Julian Weidler, contributed to the bond drive that followed, but in 1948 Judaism in the Napa Valley was practically an oxymoron. The closest Torah was in the next county; local Zionism was anemic at best, and there were hardly any Jews.

*   *   *

Except for New York and a few other major American cities, Jews were rare in most places, even where there once had been thriving Jewish communities. The hot Algerian port of Oran, for example, had been home to a lively Jewish quarter for centuries. Members of the Rouas family had lived there for five generations and had participated fully in the city's rich Jewish life.[59] They were Sephardim, with Spanish and Portuguese roots that went back to the Golden Era before 1492.

France began the conquest of Algeria in the 1830s, a process that took several decades, and by 1902 the huge expanse of mostly desert became fully French. In 1934 the Nazis instigated a deadly pogrom in the Algerian city of Constantine, and the Rouas' feared that things would get worse. Hoping for a better life, they moved to France in 1938. When German tanks rolled down the Champs Elysees, however, not even Paris was safe. The family returned to Oran.

By the time the war ended, both of Claude Rouas' parents had died, and his older brother Armand was left in charge of the family, which now had six children. Claude roamed free, a street urchin in the Algerian city of Oran.

At Armand's suggestion, Claude left Oran when he was fourteen and enrolled in a hotel and restaurant school in Algiers, where there was more opportunity to escape the poverty that now gripped the family. It was the first time he had experienced formal classroom education. He stayed there two years and graduated at the top of his class, despite an anti-Semitic teacher who despised him. With his diploma in hand, he took a job in the finest hotel in Algiers.

He began his compulsory service in the French Army in 1953, and because of his prior training he was assigned to a 5-Star General, as a butler. He traveled extensively and was discharged in Paris when the eighteen-month tour of duty ended.

The Meurice Hotel hired him, first as a busboy, then as a waiter. The Meurice experience gave him the credentials to apply for work at a top restaurant in London, the Mirabelle; and with that post on his resume he was then offered a position in one of the world's finest, Maxim's in Paris. It was demanding but rather glamorous work, and the glamour was enhanced by a relationship that developed between Claude and a movie actress, Bella Darvi. Bella was a Polish concentration camp survivor who had caught the eye of a Hollywood producer.

The owner of Ernie's restaurant in San Francisco was hoping to import Claude to California. The former street urchin and the actress, lovers now, came to the US together in 1958, and while Bella shot the movie in Hollywood, Claude worked in San Francisco. They spent the weekends together and finally married in Las Vegas.

Being a Sephardic Jew, Claude demanded from the day they married, that they would live his life, not hers. That meant managing on his salary as a waiter, not hers as a movie star. The marriage lasted six months. Bella returned to France.

* * *

Elsewhere in California, vintner Hanns (Kornblum) Kornell had tried to re-establish himself in what was left of the American wine industry. He found work in San Jose at the now-defunct Fountaingrove Winery. Champagne, however, was his primary passion. He managed to attract the interest of Cook's Imperial

Champagne Cellars in St. Louis, who offered him work at their facility in St. Louis. Laboring for another in the trade that had brought esteem to his family for generations was not quite good enough: He wanted his own company, and he wanted it to be in California, which had, he knew, the best vineyard land in America. Living very frugally, he eventually rounded up enough money to return to California and, with the help of the bank, he started a small champagne cellar in Sonoma. He did most of the labor himself and lived quietly in a room he rented at the Swiss Hotel.

Paul Vernier, the owner and president of the City of Paris department store in San Francisco, gave Hanns the break he needed by placing a big order that would guarantee wide exposure for his champagne. Vernier would do the same for other Jews in the wine business, notably Alfred Fromm, Franz Sichel and Sam Bronfman, who together had bought the Paul Masson Winery.

Lou Gomberg's business acumen also directly benefited the Napa Valley's up-and-coming wine industry. Partner in the consulting firm of Gomberg Frederikson, Gomberg identified Napa Valley wines as a special group within the industry[60] and started tracking wine production and sales, thus providing critical marketing information for Valley wineries. In 1948 he helped to found the California Wine Institute. Although not a resident of the Napa Valley, (neither were Fromm, Sichel nor Bronfman) Gomberg was one of its biggest fans and a strong promoter of the concept of quality over quantity.

*   *   *

To the egg ranchers Fred and Bella Rosenthal, "quality" would have been running a kosher home, but their efforts had failed. Young Lottie, protected as ever from the slings of prejudice, lived happily among the Italian Catholics who dominated the Napa school system. She attended Hebrew classes and received instruction in Judaism at the synagogue in Vallejo, but she found the material boring and promptly forgot what she had learned.

In 1950, when she was twenty-two, Lottie traveled cross-country to visit an aunt and her cousins in Washington Heights, a Jewish enclave in the upper part of Manhattan. It was a trip that would have huge consequences for the Jews of the Napa Valley.

It was the first time since leaving Germany that Lottie had been in a truly Jewish environment. She went to Orthodox services, where prayer shawls were worn, and the men sat downstairs while the women sat above. Everyone spoke Yiddish. She found it all quite fascinating and foreign.

Her aunt lived in an apartment complex that housed a deli. The deli was run by three brothers named Rosenberg who had come to America on the last boat of Jews to leave Italy before the ports were shut to refugees. The Rosenbergs found safety in New York and a welcome among the Orthodox Jews who had preceded them there.

Something of a matchmaker, Lottie's aunt had decided to fix her up with one of the Rosenberg boys, although not the one whom Lottie herself had noticed. George Rosenberg had also spied Lottie, who seemed out of place in Washington Heights with her Napa accent and rural ways. He called her his "little *shiksa*," a not-altogether complimentary term meaning "a Christian girl;" and he liked her a lot. When she returned to California, they started writing. The literary courtship resulted in a proposal of marriage the next year.

Orthodox George came to the Napa Valley to marry Lottie and found it to be as culturally different from his Washington Heights apartment world as a place could be. He didn't like it. He missed New York. He wanted to go back. Lottie and he agreed that they would remain in Napa for a while and then try Manhattan for a while.

By August of 1953 they were still in Napa and Lottie had just given birth to their first child. The High Holy Days were coming, and the little family was preparing to go to San Francisco, where they would attend services. Suddenly Lottie put her foot down. "I am not going to San Francisco for the High Holy Days with a new-born and staying in a hotel," she proclaimed. "Period."

To appease her, Bella suggested that they arrange to hold services as they had done before the war, in stores and private homes,
wherever space was available. Bella suggested that George, with
his solid Jewish background and training, could conduct them.
George balked at first, but finally he agreed. They called the
Baylinsons and all the other stalwart Jewish families they knew,
procured a Torah from the synagogue in Vallejo, and convened at
Joe Lazarus's auto supply company.

George Rosenberg proved to be a catalyst. With him to lead
them, the Jews of Napa once again had something they could call a
congregation. Their togetherness would create, they hoped, a place
of peace and refuge. They would be Congregation Beth Sholom,
"CBS," using the Orthodox spelling for "House of Peace." They
met at Lazarus' store and at the Napa Chamber of Commerce building for the next two years.

Present at CBS' official incorporation meeting (its birth, so to
speak) was a dignified rabbi from Germany who was now teaching
Philosophy and Humanities at Napa Valley College: Rabbi Leo
Trepp. Rabbi Trepp and his wife Miriam had left war-torn England
in a ship that was part of a convoy. During the sixteen-day trans-
Atlantic journey, their accompanying destroyer sank a German sub-
marine.

Leo was in Berkeley when he received a phone call from Harry
McPherson, the visionary president of Napa Valley College. "I
want you not in spite of your being a rabbi, but because you are
one," McPherson told him. "And perhaps your hiring will influence
the Jewish community to become a constructive part of the community [as a whole]."

The Napa Chamber of Commerce building was a mission-style
stucco structure that had outlived its usefulness in a downtown
Napa that was trying to renovate itself after decades of decay. The
city was willing to part with it for free, provided the new owners
paid for the cost of removal. Against Rabbi Trepp's advice (he

thought it was too shabby), CBS took the building and for about $2,500 in moving fees gave it a new address: 1455 Elm Street, across from Shearer Elementary School. The congregation spiffed it up later by adding a wing and transforming the exterior. To encourage participation, membership at CBS cost a mere $25 per family, at least in the beginning. (The rabbi was able to convince them to charge more than the $1.50 per month that was originally proposed.)

Buttressed, perhaps, by the validation of their reviving spiritual lives, several CBS members made polite but strong statements in the Napa community about the low level of consciousness they encountered regarding anti-Semitism. Rough Rider's Julian Weidler became president of the local Anti-Defamation League, an arm of B'nai B'rith intended to combat bias. He recognized that institutional prejudice was contrary to the spirit of the Constitution and thus illegal. Weidler was able to subtly discourage overt anti-Semitism in several venues while continuing to enjoy elected positions among persons of all faiths.[61]

Wesley Meyer also succeeded in raising public consciousness about the value of multiethnic diversity. As a member (and later president) of the Napa Kiwanis Club, for example, he could not fail to notice that the invocation prayers ended with "in the name of Jesus, our Lord." Perhaps, he pointed out to the membership, not everyone in the club was Christian. No less diplomatic than he had been when he met the Pope, he was able to alter the invocation's ending to "in the name of God," which was acceptable to the largely Christian membership because of their belief that Jesus was, in fact, God.

Meyers Jewelers continued to thrive under Wes's guidance throughout the 1950s. Wes opened branch stores in Fairfield, Vacaville, Petaluma and Santa Rosa. When the first large discount chains came into being in Northern California, he chose one and opened a jewelry department in their Stockton, Modesto and San Raphael facilities.

By 1956 his businesses were so demanding that he knew he needed to hire an experienced associate. He found the man he was looking for managing jewelry stores in New Jersey: Orville Cohen. But while Orville and Wes became best of friends and trusted associates, it was Orville's wife and especially her father who had the most unique impact on the fledgling congregation.

Alice Muscatine Cohen had been an actress in her hometown of Trenton.[62] She had performed in plays and had worked at a small NBC affiliate, WTTN, with an up-and-coming Jewish comedian named Ernie Kovaks. She was also the president of the Trenton Council of Jewish Women, a sisterhood that engaged in charitable work. She helped to organize a similar group for Beth Sholom. Hardly the retiring type, she joined the Pretenders drama group and took the stage in a variety of theatrical performances.

When Alice and Orville left Trenton to start new lives in Napa at Meyers Jewelers, Alice's parents were disconsolate. They, too, moved to Napa, arriving in 1958. For Alice's father, coming to Napa was the final point of a journey that had taken him halfway around the world.

Sam Mushkatin was the youngest of seven children who lived crammed together in a small dwelling in the *shtetl* of Orsha, White Russia, a town no longer on the map. The *shtetl* was on ground owned by the Catholic Church, which protected the Jews there from violence by their Christian neighbors. One by one the Mushkatin children managed to slip away to America, where they got jobs and sent money back home for the rest. One night in 1903, twelve-year-old Sam left his mother and father and fled with another family through meadows and forests until they came to the seaport of St. Petersburg. He boarded a ship and, traveling in steerage, he eventually came to New York and somehow reunited with his sister, a seamstress. As Sam Muscatine, he worked and learned English, staying up late at night reading the classics.

Like so many before him, Sam became a "traveling salesman" (i.e. a peddler). His route took him through the rural countryside of

Upstate New York. One summer during World War I, while he was hawking products "made in Japan" to vacationers in the Catskills, Sam met Bertha Greenberg, the lovely daughter of a prosperous woolen merchant. Her father had been trying to marry her off to a succession of fat, cigar-puffing merchants, but she had so far managed to resist. Sam proved to be the best salesman of all, and by the end of the war they were married. They had three children.[63]

The addition of the Muscatines went a long way toward stabilizing Congregation Beth Sholom. Sam was deeply rooted in Orthodox Judaism and became a close friend and indispensable assistant to George Rosenberg, serving as Sexton. Things would remain this way for a long time, with George and Sam in leadership positions, a few families doing much of the volunteer work and Rough Rider executives like Danny Weinstein and Julian Weidler donating liberally to the coffers. Rabbi Trepp served as an advisor and consultant to CBS and became its part-time rabbi in 1961.

Fundraisers were easy. Rough Rider donated unsold merchandise to the synagogue's annual Rummage Sale, and the proceeds sometimes came to as much as $25,000 a day, with frenzied bargain-shoppers hauling off bags full of premium merchandise for a song.

Jews who might fill the little synagogue at worship services also began to trickle into Napa. Some liked what they saw at CBS. Some didn't.

Chapter Ten

The man asked him, "What is your name?"
"Jacob," he answered.
Then the man said, "Your name will no longer be
Jacob, but Israel, because you have struggled with
God and with men and have overcome." —Genesis 32:28-30

THE JEWS HAVE HAD NO MORE SUCCESS AGREEING ON HOW TO PROP-
erly worship the Divine than the Christians (Protestant vs. Catholic)
or the Muslims (Sunni vs. Shiite). When Rome destroyed the second temple, the Pharisees, Sadducees, Essenes and Zealots were all
at odds; two millennia later Jews still wrestle with God and with
each other over matters of theology.

Orthodox Jews believe that God gave the Torah to Moses, and
they endeavor to adhere to the Biblical laws. Many ultra-Orthodox
even try to limit their contact with the outside world. But
Orthodoxy demands that one be able to walk to *shul* and observe a
kosher diet, difficult for folks in rural communities like Napa, as
Bella Rosenthal discovered. Thus true Orthodox Judaism flourish-
es best in small urban pockets similar to the *shtetls* and ghettos in
which it originally developed. Originally Orthodox, George
Rosenberg and Sam Muscatine couldn't maintain their Orthodoxy
in Napa.

Conservative Jews try to keep kosher, observe Shabbat and the

Jewish holidays and engage in an active daily prayer life, but they often regard many of the restrictions of Orthodoxy to be irrelevant and culture-bound. Conservatives feel that the *halachah*, the religious laws, are open to interpretation.

Reform Judaism grew from a desire on the part of German Jews to blend in more with the surrounding society. Many of the Jews who came to California during the Gold Rush were Reform. This branch of Judaism urges believers to be like Jacob and wrestle for themselves with matters of spiritual practice and belief. They use the Torah, the *halachah*, and everything else traditionally Jewish, as guides for— but not dictators of—belief. Reform Jews thus feel somewhat hemmed in when in Orthodox or Conservative settings, while Orthodox and Conservatives find Reform Judaism lacking in the richness of tradition at best, and at worst, barely Jewish at all.

There are other, smaller branches on the Jewish tree. Reconstructionist Jews see the universe as constantly in the state of being created, and Jews as responsible for assisting God in the ongoing work by helping to bring order out of the chaos of the as-yet-uncreated. Spiritual practice, to be vital, must be fluid, forever changing, they believe. Rabbi David Kopstein, part-time CBS rabbi for eight years before being called to a synagogue in New Zealand, was Reconstructionist.

Somewhat less heady is the philosophy of Renewal Jews, who encourage their congregations to draw from diverse sources such as contemporary psychology, Eastern religions, and relevant socio-political movements like feminism and environmentalism to create *chavurot*, small groups of friends who study together and explore new liturgical directions.

Messianic Jews believe that Christ was the Messiah and await Jesus' return: a position that causes most other Jews to doubt whether they are Jews at all. One of the children of CBS co-founder Joe Lazarus became a member of "Jews for Jesus," a phrase that is mutually exclusive to most Jews but seems less so to evangelical

Christians.

Secular Humanistic Jews identify themselves as culturally, genetically and psychologically Jewish but see God as either non-existent or so ineffable and uninvolved in human affairs as to be of negligible relevance to human beings. Many Jews in the Napa Valley (and elsewhere) see themselves as secular and have minimal contact with the liturgical elements of Judaism, although they still identify themselves as Jewish.

How could one little synagogue serve such diversity of belief? It couldn't. CBS became more or less a Conservative congregation with strong Orthodox overtones, as suited the tastes of George Rosenberg and the other founders, as well as the practicalities of the location. Newcomers who could relate to this slant fit in well.

The Tannenbaums, for example, fit in fine, although it might have been difficult for people to keep track of all the names in the family.[64] The son, Chaim, was born in Russia in 1940. Originally Polish, his mother (Luba Abramowicz) moved to the small Russian city of Penza when the German Army sent his father to fight on the Russian front. His father never returned. Chaim spent part of his childhood in a Displaced Persons' camp in Germany, where his mother married Joshua Tannenbaum. Chaim kept his father's name: He was Chaim Abramowicz.

The new family immigrated to the United States. The intake officer at Ellis Island convinced Chaim that his name would be a problem for him, so she changed it for him. Now he was "Harvey Abramowicz." The family kept traveling west and found a home in San Francisco, in the Fillmore District.

The Tannenbaums discovered that another family of Jewish refugees lived upstairs. Former displaced persons Joseph and Fela (now Felicia) Michalski had endured the two-week boat trip to New York and grappled for a year with East Coast weather. Not intimidated by long distances, this family who had walked from Kazakhstan to Bavaria took the train to San Francisco and settled in the tough Fillmore neighborhood. The Tannenbaums, Michalskis and Harvey Abramowicz spoke Yiddish at home and took classes to improve their English

In 1954 Joshua Tannenbaum bought "Oscar's Junkyard" near the intersection of Tannen and Soscol Streets in Napa and changed his own first name to "Oscar." The family lived at the junkyard, which was also renamed: It became the Tannen Family Junkyard.

After he graduated from Napa High, Harvey went to work in a hardware store in San Francisco, where he met, courted and soon married a girl from the Bronx, Myrna Landau. Myrna's first trip to Napa was to meet her in-laws-to-be, and it was almost the last she took anywhere. She got out of the car to get a close-up look at the cows grazing in a pasture just south of town—she'd never seen a bovine up close. This raised the ire of a nearby bull, which charged at her à la Pamplona, while she ran for her life.

Harvey and Myrna Abramowicz became central figures at CBS. He was principal of the Sunday School and taught Hebrew; she served as president of the Sisterhood, taught history and started the local Hadassah chapter. Harvey died of leukemia a decade later. Myrna drew upon her own deep well of personal courage and started over. She eventually became very active in local politics: a turn of events she would never have imagined on that first trip to Napa.

Morris and Annie Nussbaum also fit in fine.[65] Morris' family had come to America from Poland when Morris was a child. He was raised in Branchville, SC, a town that happened to have many Jewish merchants. Branchville was on the train route to Charleston, South Carolina, but Morris's father and uncle, who were looking for work together, thought they were heading for Charleston, West Virginia and took the wrong train. As God (or fate, or random chance, depending on one's religious slant) would have it, they happened to step off in Branchville and immediately ran into another Jew, an event that convinced them to lay down roots right there.

The Nussbaums had three children, Rachel, Minnie and Harris, and the family eventually moved out west. In searching for a small, comfortable community in which to live, they discovered Napa, a homey spot that reminded them a little of Branchville. Morris bought a failing enterprise called Euster's (also owned by a Jewish family) and renamed it "Brewster's," because he wanted it to be near the front of the telephone book.

The original Brewster's resembled a peddler's pack. Morris sold a hodge-podge of items, including surplus from the Korean War and assorted articles of clothing, especially men's. It reflected Morris' own career, during which he was textile wholesaler, had furniture stores, dabbled in the oil business and worked in an Army-Navy surplus store.

Harris Nussbaum went to work for his father, and Rachel married a Jew who also had Polish roots, Larry Friedman, who happened to operate an Army-Navy surplus store on Market Street in San Francisco. In 1960, Morris and the Friedmans decided to trade stores. The plan worked beautifully for the Friedmans, who turned Brewster's into a very successful retail operation, and well for the elder Nussbaums; but it didn't suit young Harris Nussbaum, who discovered that he really didn't like sales at all. Harris went on to become a high school teacher and established a cutting-edge peer-counseling program at Vintage High School. Minnie left the area but eventually returned and also became a teacher, giving new hope to disabled children.

Like Morris, Rachel and Larry became very involved in CBS. The philosophy there, they learned, was "don't make waves." There was no interfaith activity, not even a Boy Scout troop. A Berkeley graduate, Rachel found this too constricting and went about trying to pry open the congregation to attempting new things. She started a Sunday School and directed a Sunday Fun Day activity that featured klezmer music, Jewish food, art and dancing on then-vacant acreage west of town. Why the congregational shyness, she wondered? Some of the members, she was told, were Holocaust survivors who didn't want to attract attention.

Psychiatrist Abe Linn and his wife Terri moved to Napa in 1961, when Abe was hired to a position at Napa State Hospital.[66] Although born Jewish, Terri's experience with Judaism had been minimal until she married Abe, whose family was observant. The couple had lived for a time in Los Angeles. There, they enjoyed intellectually stimulating dialogue with their Jewish friends. They hoped for the same thing in Napa. When they first stepped foot in the synagogue at Beth Sholom, however, Terri felt as though she were being examined under a microscope. Acquaintances whom she had known about town seemed cool toward her, and she felt uninspired to return.

The Linns' problems were compounded by an incident that occurred one winter about two years after they arrived, when their six-year-old son came home from his first grade class and asked, "Why is Jesus our savior?" Terri went to the boy's teacher and explained that although the family enjoyed Christmas carols as music, teaching him that Jesus would save him was against the family's religion. The teacher became defensive and was close to tears; she later told the principal, who consulted the city attorney. Abe went to the school and again explained the family's position.

The Linns thought the matter was resolved until an account of it appeared on the front page of the *Napa Register* with a banner headline that said, "Christmas Programs Ruled OK," with a smaller headline adding that "Area Schools Will Not Cancel Plans," as if the Linns, like the Grinch, somehow intended to steal Christmas.[67] The story quoted Abe Linn as saying, "My feeling is that religious training or programs are unconstitutional. I questioned the program only on a legal basis. I am not objecting on a religious basis." Dr. Linn, the *Register* article said, would consult an attorney to see whether he wanted to take legal action. Moreover, the story said that "a man identifying himself as Linn telephoned the county counsel and stated that if the opinion did not prohibit the Christmas program, he would 'take the school into the federal courts'."

Dan York, the city attorney, issued a statement with the opinion that "public schools may present a Christmas program so long as such selections are not used for religious purposes."

The story went out over the wire services and sparked an outrage. Not only did the Linns receive hate mail from strangers around the country as a result of the publicity, but, even worse, some local Jews telephoned warning them not to make waves. "It's too close in time to the Holocaust," they were told. "Don't do anything to put Jewish people in danger."

Abe went on to be the Medical Director of Napa State Hospital, and Terri became a prominent Napa family counselor. They did not become supporting members of CBS, although they attended occasionally.

While there was no physical danger to the Jews in the Napa Valley in the 1950s and '60s, there was clear emotional peril. With traumatized Holocaust survivors on one side and xenophobic gentiles on the other, it was hard for some Jews to feel entirely safe.

One family who managed to steer a safe middle course were the Percelays. Also a mental health professional, psychiatrist Eliot Percelay brought his wife Anne, a teacher, and their two sons to the Napa Valley in 1962. One of the first things Anne did before buying a home was to call the synagogue to be assured of a Jewish community. She spoke with George Rosenberg, who performed many of the pastoral duties there and in many ways was the voice of the congregation. Over the years Anne taught Sunday School, served as president of the Sisterhood and president of Hadassah. She also taught Hebrew to adults.[68]

In the mid-1970s CBS member Henry Michalski invited Anne to lecture about Judaism to his high school class. She spoke mainly about holidays and rituals. When one young student suddenly realized that as a Jew, Anne didn't believe that Jesus is God, she

Barntrup, Germany, circa 1920: Egon Katz, the baby, would survive the horrors of World War II, as would his brothers, but his sisters would not. He began a new life in America as Eugene Katz.

Rough Rider made major contributions to the economy of Napa and to the well-being of Congregation Beth Sholom. L-R Dan Weinstein, Morton Rothman, Julian Weidler, Bert Margolis, and Dan Broverman. Nat Rothman (insert) founded Rough Rider and brought it to Napa in 1936 during the Great Depression.

Displaced persons arrived in America on ships after WWII. Seen steaming into port here is the Freihafen, *which brought the Michalskis to the US.*

Joseph Michalski was captured by the Russians and sent to a POW camp at Sobieski Castle in Olesko, a city in the Ukraine. He wrote to his girlfriend, Fela, and convinced her to join him there. They married. Below, Fela and toddler Henry Michalski in a Displaced Persons' camp. Photos courtesy of Henry Michalski.

Lost at sea: Harold Levy, a Levinson descendant, perished aboard the Neosho *during World War II.*

Wesley and Ellie Meyer

Photo courtesy of Ellie Meyer

Lieutenant Wesley Meyer

The Napa Valley's very first Bar Mitzvah was in 1953. Lay leader George Rosenberg is flanked by Bernard Gordon (left), son of George and Shirley Gordon, and Norman (right), son of Ilya "Chick" and Rose Gordon.

Alfred Fromm (second from left), Franz Sichel (second from right) with Norman Fromm (right) and a Christian Brothers executive.

Zoltan and Sara Rosenberger's new Goodman's Department Store amazed St. Helenans with its wealth of merchandise and good prices when it opened in 1961.

Photo courtesy of Zoltan Rosenberger

Many at Congregation Beth Sholom considered the synagogue part of a Jewish Community Center. The addition of a swimming pool in 1963 pleased some, upset others.

Napa Register, *5-31-1963*

Photo courtesy of Dona Kopol Bonick

Joe Lazarus

burst into tears, overwhelmed with the fear that Anne wouldn't be "saved."

Donna and Ernie Heine ran into some gentiles with emotions of a different sort.[69] A transfer at Ernie's work brought them to Napa on Mother's Day in 1962 with their eleven-year-old daughter, Nancy. Donna was nine months pregnant. They checked the phone book and saw the listing for CBS. Sunday School was in session, and they found John Marx and George Rosenberg, Joe Lazarus and a Rough Rider executive, "Chick" Gordon, there. The men gave the Heines a warm welcome, and even helped them find a house to buy.

It was at the title company, while they were signing the papers for their Napa home, that the Heines received the first sign that not everyone in Napa was liberal-minded. They asked the loan officer if she knew of anyone who could do housecleaning for her. The woman told them, "There are no n----'s here."

That was the beginning of the Heines' experiences with prejudice in the Napa Valley. More followed. When young Nancy had to miss school in the sixth grade because of the High Holy Days, she gave the teacher a note explaining her absence. A change came over the teacher, subtle at first, and then increasingly apparent. Things came to a head when the class was studying geography. While the rest of the class was invited to focus on any country they chose, Nancy was told to work on Israel, "because that's your country."

"No," said Nancy, "Israel is not my country, I want to select another one." The teacher insisted. Finally, Nancy told her parents she didn't want to go to school anymore.

Donna spoke with the teacher twice and was told both times that Nancy was the only Jewish student in the class, "so she needs to excel, to be the top student." Concerned, Ernie and Donna scheduled an appointment with the principal, the teacher, the school counselor and the Dean of Girls. The teacher reasserted her position: "Nancy's my only Jewish student," she said, and because Nancy was Jewish she had to be the top student in the class. The teacher may never have realized the bigotry behind her thinking, but the principal did. He apologized to the Heines and had the school counselor immediately reassign Nancy to a different class-room.

Later when the Heines went to build a new home in an upscale section of town, they encountered a full dose of anti-Semitic bias. Their architect wanted to nestle the house in the existing environment, among some fine old trees. The ecologically sensitive plan required a two-foot variance so that the dwelling could be situated below the proposed driveway. Two hours before the Planning Commission was scheduled to meet to OK the variance, the Heines received a troubled telephone call from Commissioner Mike Joel informing them that there was a petition to block the variance.

The Heines rushed to the meeting. One by one, their future neighbors rose to speak on how the variance would ruin the view and harm the trees. "I'm sorry," said the wealthy neighbor who led the protest; "I hope you understand." Donna understood only too well that the petition had nothing to do with trees and the two-foot variance.

The incident left her furious and downright ill.

The next day, another member of the Planning Commission called to say that the members had decided to grant the variance despite the petition. Completely soured to the prospect of living among such neighbors, the Heines dropped thier request. Donna and Ernie sold the property and wrote a letter to all those in their would-be neighborhood who did not sign the petition, thanking them for their kindness.

Having been present at its birth and an adviser for ten years, Rabbi Leo Trepp became CBS' first part-time rabbi in 1961. Rabbi Trepp was very involved in the community at large and attempted to bridge the gap between the "don't make waves" members and their environment. Several times, for instance, he invited a quartet at Pacific Union College to come to the synagogue and perform.

The concerts were packed, but rarely with Jews.

The foyer at CBS contained memorial tablets donated by members to honor deceased loved ones. The names on the tablets were written in Hebrew, and some had misspellings and erroneous dates: a problem for those wanting to light candles to remember the deceased. The author of several books on Judaism and an expert in Hebrew, the scholarly Trepp offered to correct the mistakes. "This is a free country," someone told him; "we can spell however we want!"

The end of Trepp's term as part-time rabbi for CBS occurred in 1963. Rabbi Trepp's supporters, many of them newcomers to the synagogue, wanted to grant him a raise in pay and utilize his expertise in educational programs. Joe Lazarus and his brother-in-law Ben Baylinson, leaders of the old guard, opposed this and managed to acquire money from "anonymous donors" (executives at Rough Rider) to build a swimming pool, instead. Their message was clear: CBS was to be a lay-led congregation, and they would be the lay leaders. The money and the controversy surrounding it drove a wedge into the congregation for a time.

Trepp left as part-time rabbi, although he remained in Napa. He also worked part-time in Santa Rosa and in Ukiah and was beloved in those places. He was a chaplain at the Veterans' Home. He taught college classes in Napa and in Solano County. He served on the Napa Planning Commission and was well known in the community both for his teaching and his leadership skills. Miriam was also a leader, enjoying a career in teaching that spanned twenty-five years in the Napa school system. A succession of rabbis interacted with CBS over the years. Until 2003 none was full-time, and none but the spurned Leo Trepp lived in Napa County.[70]

Some of the members followed Leo Trepp out the door. One of those to depart was Alvin "Lee" Block, MD, an Internist with a large practice who was a great admirer of the rabbi.[71] Lee had been president of the congregation for a term and enjoyed involving himself with other Jews. He felt welcomed and very comfortable in the small congregation. But when his co-religionists chose the swimming pool over education and the rabbi, he lost his enthusiasm for Congregation Beth Sholom. He would later make a substantial contribution through the Jewish Community of the Napa Valley, which he helped to found, but after the swimming pool incident his appearances at CBS were limited to High Holy Days and other special occasions.

Dr. Block practiced medicine with his brother Rodney, a Nephrologist, for thirty-five years, and their contribution to local medicine was considerable. Rodney began dialysis services in the Napa Valley. He put together the area's first dialysis machine, ran both acute and chronic dialysis services for Queen of the Valley Hospital and eventually began his own dialysis unit. Together the Block Brothers served as coordinators for planning at the hospital, conducted physician teaching programs, and created the first Intensive Care Unit (ICU) there.[72]

Lee Block's interests extended far beyond the examining room. When he learned that the Southern Pacific Railroad was selling its short lines, for example, he gathered a group of investors to join him in buying what had been the Napa Valley Railroad. They sold the line to Vincent and Mildred DeDomenico, who turned it into the Napa Valley Wine Train.

*   *   *

What few Jews there were in the Napa Valley in the 1960s lived mainly in the city of Napa. The second largest city in the valley, St. Helena, had by now no or hardly any Jews, and none who regularly practiced the faith. Joe Galewsky, the Jewish postmaster who started life as a little rascal, ended it as a friend to all in 1959. He inherited the family stationery business and ran it successfully for sixty years.[73] He was a charter member of the St. Helena Rotary Club, a Mason and a Native Son of the Golden West. The local Masonic lodge organized his funeral. A rabbi from San Francisco's

Sherith Israel officiated, but none of the pallbearers was Jewish.

Leopold Lazarus had long since passed on, and none of his family remained in St. Helena. His son Sylvain had enjoyed a successful career as a lawyer and eventually became a judge in the Superior Court in San Francisco. Sylvain and his wife (Rosalind Schneider of Marysville) had a son they named Leland, whose career was also stellar. Leland had served a stint as a reporter for a San Francisco newspaper, was appointed as a field administrator for FDR's National Recovery Administration, and eventually became a lawyer and a judge. He served on the San Francisco Board of Education, was a member of the Democratic Central Committee and an officer of several Jewish and secular organizations.

Goodman's department store was still the largest clothing retailer in town, but original owner Abraham Goodman was dead, as were his sons Julius and Jacob. Julius had become interested in politics—not as a Democrat, but as a Republican, which made him a bit of an anomaly for a Jew at that time. With little or no reinforcement for his Judaic roots, his primary identity was as a small businessman in a rural community. His brother Jacob married a Christian woman, Katie, who continued the business after Jacob passed away in 1956.

Into this sleepy little village drove, one day, two Hungarian-Mexican-Jews looking for the road to Santa Rosa. Zoltan and Sara Rosenberger had finally relinquished their shoe store in Baja and moved to California with at least enough for the down payment on a new business. Sara liked the quiet, unpretentious town, which in 1961 seemed sound asleep. So little traffic disturbed its broad Main Street that children roller-skated down the middle of it, while dogs lazed in the sunshine on the sidewalks. Sara had Zoltan pull the car to the curb in front of a real estate agency for an informal inquiry into what might be available there.

The agent excused himself and ran across the street. A few minutes later he returned with elderly Katie Goodman in tow.

Would they like to come look at the department store? She'd been hoping to sell it for some time, with no luck. Zoltan knew about luck. Good fortune (or perhaps God Himself) now seemed to be smiling on him. Zoltan and Sara eagerly accepted and bought it on the spot.

What they found was a place that hadn't been updated since the 1880s, when Abe Goodman won the war of the Jewish merchants. The shelves were dusty and nearly barren, the floors needed to be replaced, the lighting was poor...it was as sad and despondent looking as Zoltan himself had seemed back when Sara first met him. Knowing what magic a little TLC could do, they spent what they had and borrowed more to modernize the place and fill its empty shelves with a broad selection of ready-to-wear clothes. It was an offering more abundant than anyone had ever seen in St. Helena, and it was an instant success.

Very soon after purchasing the place, Zoltan made a networking call to Rough Rider, where he introduced himself and struck a deal to sell their apparel at reduced prices that would please everyone. He and Sara also joined CBS: the first time they had been active in Judaism since leaving Cluj. Their attendance was infrequent (although Zoltan served briefly as Vice President of the congregation), but it was good to gather with Jews again.

The Rosenbergers were almost the only Jews in St. Helena, but not quite. Far to the north, near the border with Calistoga, Hanns (Kornblum) Kornell had bought the old Salmina Winery on Larkmead Lane. It was a lovely old stone building, although not nearly so grand as the place his family had known in Germany. He and his wife Marilouise (an Italian Swiss, like the Salminas had been) also bought acreage that once belonged to her grandfather, and there they built a home.

To finance these purchases, Hanns worked out a loan with Andy Johnson, president of the local Bank of America. Johnson and the bank were very supportive of the wine industry. It was a deal sealed with a handshake. Hanns, Andy, the mayor, a few other winemakers and one or two of the town's other worthies met for breakfast each morning, shot the breeze, chewed the fat, and watched the grass grow. On the side he also made excellent champagne and soon, money.

In 1965, when the California Wine Institute first hired him as a consultant, future St. Helenan Harvey Posert began bringing wine writers to the Napa Valley. Institute president Harry Serlis (also born Jewish) warned Harvey to "be careful:" there were hardly any Jews in Napa County.[74]

Harvey Posert's family tree has Sephardic roots. J.J. Peres, great-great-grandfather on his mother's side, arrived in America around 1850 from Holland, but the Peres family had lived for generations in Portugal, and before 1492 in Spain. The first American Posert was a Polish doctor who stepped off the boat at Ellis Island in the 1890s and found his way to the river town of Memphis, home to the large Jewish population described earlier.

Harvey attended Sunday School at a Reform synagogue but found religion classes to be boring and anti-intellectual. Like his father, he attended Yale under the anti-Semitic quota system and left as a Secular Humanist with little interest in God but a strong Jewish identity nevertheless. His writing career brought him into a milieu that has always been a Jewish specialty: adviser to the crown, which in modern terms translates as "public relations."

His first need as an easterner freshly arrived on the West Coast was to find housing. While a friend was driving him around in Marin County to look at homes, Harvey asked, "Where do the Jews live?" "All over," he was told. To Harvey this was a new concept. East Coast Jews routinely experienced being ushered to areas where Jews were already present while being excluded from other parts of town (indeed, certain towns were notorious for having Boards of Realtors who actively discouraged Jews from moving into the community at all). Moreover, as discussed above, Orthodox Jews needed to group near a *shul* in order to walk to services. The distribution of Jews in California thus reflected not only California's tendency to fair-minded heterogeneity, but also its relative scarcity of Orthodox Jews. Coarse anti-Semitism such as the Heines experienced verged on the unusual for Californians.

Harvey concluded that there are really two different kinds of anti-Semitism. There is ignorant, perhaps unintentional prejudice, where people with little exposure to Jews express a degree of xenophobia, like the secretary who commented to one of his Jewish associates that having a Jewish boss would "be interesting," as if Jews were some other, slightly different life form. The other kind of anti-Semitism is conscious hate. Expressions like "those kike distributors" are of this ilk, or being told that another Jew is "your relative" because of his Judaism. He found examples of both varieties of prejudice while working in the wine industry (the former more dominant than the latter), but on the whole Harvey has found the Napa Valley to be a comfortable and satisfying place to live.[75]

Dormant as it had been for so long, the wine business was showing hints of recovery in the 1960s. One sign was the unprecedented success of the Christian Brothers Winery. Thanks in large part to Fromm & Sichel (of which the Bronfman family owned 70%) Christian Brothers products were sold in every state and in sixty foreign countries. Their hard work and the Brothers' product were crucial in opening up the wine market to the middle class.[76]

After snatching his family from the clutches of the Nazis, Alfred Fromm turned his attention to other forms of philanthropy. Along with his wife Hanna, he founded the Fromm Institute for Lifelong Learning at the University of San Francisco, a "university within a university" offering classes taught by retired professors to students in their fifties or older. Three dozen or so were expected to enroll the first day. Five hundred people showed up.[77]

Alfred Fromm and Hanns Kornell came from families who had been in the business for generations. Other Jews with far less experience found themselves in the Napa Valley's re-emerging wine industry in the 1960s.

While they were dating, Federal Trade Commission lawyer Michael Bernstein and his wife-to-be Arlene had discovered and fallen in love with the remote and woodsy wilds of Mount Veeder, near the county's western boundary.[78] In 1964 Michael read an ad in the *Wall Street Journal* describing a prune orchard for sale there. They bought it and spent their downtime in a rustic cottage that came with the property. One day, a farm worker who had helped with the prune harvest brought them a stack of vine cuttings. On Memorial Day, 1965, they stuck the canes, one by one, in what had been the cow pasture. Amazingly, of fifty-eight cuttings, fifty-six survived, without even being irrigated.

Sadly, the Bernsteins' cozy existence was rocked by a series of personal disasters. The death of two infants plunged Michael and Arlene into a period of deep grieving. In 1971 Michael withdrew from his demanding job at the FTC, and the couple moved into the cabin that had been their hide-away. They made a living sharing one job as a tour guide at Robert Mondavi Winery, which was still in its infancy.

By 1977 the prune orchard was a memory. The Bernsteins' vineyard, planted vine by vine, now featured a selection of premium Bordeaux varietals: Cabernet Sauvignon, Merlot, Cabernet Franc, Malbec and Petite Verdot. What had begun as a romantic whim was showing signs of becoming a serious endeavor.

Michael healed his grief by devoting himself to the vineyard and winemaking. Arlene worked in the garden and became absorbed in nature's miracles of growth, death, and regeneration: realities that had touched her so deeply. Through meditation, she was eventually able to create a kind of order out of the chaos that had befallen the family. Nourished and strengthened by the soils of Mount Veeder, Arlene went on to become a family counselor and eventually wrote a book, *Growing Season*, describing how they transformed the land while it, in turn, transformed them.

The Bernsteins' Mount Veeder wines turned out to be power-ful, dramatic vintages full of mint and berry flavors. Wine critic Jim Laube hailed their 1973 one of the top five or six Cabernets pro-duced that year.

Michael decided that to even further improve his skills, he would join the Napa Valley Vintners' Association. He called to inquire, but the spokesperson there didn't respond right away. Finally he told Michael, "The membership isn't really open. If we considered someone like you, then we'd have to let in people like Al Brounstein and others like him." Michael, Al, and Hanns Kornell were the only Jewish winemakers in the valley at that time, and Hanns did not reveal his background to many.

Like the Bernsteins, Albert Jack Brounstein, known to all as "Al," knew little about the wine industry before he came to the Napa Valley. Al was never one to be deterred by a challenge. It was Al's father, Harry, who sold liquor on the sly for Sam Bronfman during Prohibition, and Al himself who conquered the streets of Minneapolis by balancing on the handlebars of bikes as a child. While the Bernsteins brought to the Valley the spiritual element of meditative awareness, Al offered another very Jewish example: that of *chutzpah*.

Chapter Eleven

I had planted you like a choice vine
of sound and reliable stock. —Jeremiah 2:21

AL BROUNSTEIN GRADUATED FROM THE UNIVERSITY OF MINNESOTA
in 1942 with a degree in business. Listed 4-F because of a stomach
problem, he headed to Los Angeles to find work. After a brief and
boring stint selling candy and later bedding at Mays Department
store, he sought something that would give him more freedom. He
hired on with a wholesaler who provided over-the-counter supplies
to drugstores, and while Al was stocking the shelves he hit upon the
idea of managing the inventories for his accounts, an innovation
that soon yielded him more than a million dollars in business.

Al wanted to take a business trip to Europe, and to prepare for
the adventure he took a wine-tasting course.

"You know," he told the instructor on the last day of class, "this
sounds like a fun way to go. I'd like to put up a little vineyard and
just sell the grapes and have a quiet, peaceful life."

"Don't do it," replied the teacher. "You'll never make any
money, you'll only lose."[79]

With these words of discouragement, the bootlegger's son set
the gentleman vintner dream on the back burner, where it simmered

quietly for a good long time. Rather than dissipate, however, the vision began to develop. Not only would he have the lovely vineyard, he mused, but he'd have the best wine, too. Nothing less than Cabernet Sauvignon would do, he decided.

Casually at first, he began to search for the perfect setting, somewhere warm and sunny, where he could fly his airplane and sail his boat while he waited for the vines to ripen and the wine to age. The balmy weather near San Diego would suit him, he decided; he started there and slowly worked his way up the coast, looking for vineyard land to buy. Cabernet, he discovered, would grow best farther north. He relinquished the sailing idea but pressed on in his quest for the ideal place to make wine.

It was at Ridge Vineyards in the Santa Cruz Mountains that Al Brounstein finally got his first experience in an actual vineyard. He flew up there from his home in Los Angeles on the weekends during crush, picked grapes, and flew home Sunday nights drenched in grape juice and wreathed in smiles. And more determined than ever to become a winegrower.

But where? Where, he asked the Santa Cruz County Farm Adviser, was the very best place to grow Cabernet Sauvignon? The Napa Valley, the Farm Advisor told him.

"Then that's where I'm going," said Al, and there he went, in 1967.[80]

One of the first people with whom he consulted was the Napa County Farm Advisor, who told him he needed to look for vineyard land in the northern part of the Valley, where it's hottest. Al also paid a visit to Beaulieu's legendary winemaker Andre Tschelistcheff, who agreed. A real estate agent found him twenty plantable acres of mostly unimproved land on Diamond Mountain in Calistoga for $1,400 an acre, and he was all set to make wine. All he needed were the vines, the winery, the equipment, the staff, and some basic education on how to be a vineyardist.

The very best grapevines in the world, he learned, grow in France. These "First Growths" are the top French vintages, also known as the Premier Cru (the likes of Chateaux Lafitte, Latour, Margaux, Haut-Brion, Mouton-Rothschild, Cheval Blanc, Ausone and Pomerol.) The State of California, however, required that the cuttings from First Growth vineyards would have to be indexed and quarantined for six years, and although Al was patient, this would not do.

The same time that Al was contemplating how to bring France's finest to California, Israeli bombers were taking off on a mission to Egypt. Egyptian President Gamal Abdel Nasser had been rattling sabres in the Sinai and had entered into an alliance with Syria for the purpose of annihilating Israel. The tiny Jewish homeland, populated largely with survivors of the Holocaust and Stalin's purges, waited in agony, dreading the worst.

Instead they got a miracle. Six days later, Israel stood in possession of territory more than twice its original size, and a people who for 2,000 years had been stepped on as the planet's perennial victims shouted *Stop!* to its persecutors. The Six Day War revealed Israel to be far superior to its military enemies and a force to be reckoned with.

Having seen first-hand the ravages of an earlier war, Henry Michalski knew in high school that he would become a history teacher. In 1968, the year that superintendent Austin Kelly first hired him to teach in Napa, Henry was fervently pro-Israel and actively against the war in Vietnam. So earnest were his objections to fighting in Vietnam that he asked Rabbi Trepp to write a letter to his draft board supporting his anti-war views. The rabbi interviewed him for hours but declined to write the letter. Jews, Trepp told him, are not pacifists, and they should honor the laws of the land in which they live. Henry got Austin Kelly to write the letter instead, and the draft board gave him an occupational deferment.

The David vs. Goliath outcome of the Six Day War inspired many an American Jew, including young Ernie Weir.[81] Like many Jewish families, Ernie's enjoyed wine, even back in the 1960s when the California wine industry was still in its post-Prohibition slumber. Although he grew up in the Los Angeles area, wine country place names like St. Helena, Rutherford and Calistoga were thus familiar to him. Ernie liked agriculture, too; he liked the concept of working with the earth to help it bring forth its abundance. After graduating from UCLA in 1971 he spent a year in a kibbutz in Israel, where he came to know the spiritual soil of his own ancestral roots and thoroughly immersed himself in Hebrew community and culture. He also got to know something about farming and, specifically, viticulture.

When his year was finished he came to the Napa Valley and joined Domaine Chandon, specializing in the propagation of grape vines. Ernie worked there for twenty-four years, from 1973 until 1997. Along the way, he met his Israeli wife Irit, a Doctor of Oriental Medicine with whom he shares his deep interest in and love for Israel. He also enrolled in the University of Davis and received a degree in viticulture. He was preparing himself for a goal which he wouldn't be able to realize for many years, but he, like all good farmers, was patient.

Al Brounstein may also have drawn inspiration from the Six Day War. Unwilling to be shackled by red tape in Sacramento, he called some friends. Which friends they were he has kept a secret, but the first was someone who sold French wine in the United States, with whom the French Premier Cru vintners were well acquainted. The second was a female intermediary who lived in Mexico.

By 1968, his French connection had convinced two of the First Growth vineyards to ship a large bundle of premium-quality cuttings to Tijuana, which did not have indexing or quarantine requirements. Al flew his small plane to a private airport at Rosarita beach, and in the dark of night his confederate there helped him smuggle the budwood into his airplane. In the morning they flew out with the canes hidden in a compartment behind the fuselage where he sometimes carried his snow skis. US customs officials never looked there.

It took seven trips. When it was all done, Al had enough First Growth cuttings to plant his vineyard. While his vines developed, he gained industry experience by working for other wineries.

It was Al's eye for detail that had made him his fortune in the drug business; the same propensity would serve him well as a wine-grower. He observed that the soils of his vineyard differed from one another. One section was red, the dirt there full of iron. Another was gray, rich in volcanic ash from eruptions some 8,000,000 years ago, when the Napa Valley was largely under water. The third section, which he planted later, was gravelly. The three soil types merged next to the creek that ran through a portion of the property. It was for this little mountain waterway that he named his enterprise Diamond Creek Winery.

When he harvested his 1972 vintage, he decided to crush the grapes from the red and the gray soils separately, and when the wines they produced were ready to drink, he invited a group of wine writers to come taste. Indeed, they said, there was a dis-cernible difference between the two. He thus labeled the small 1972 vintage "Volcanic Hill" and "Red Rock Terrace." When he finally harvested grapes from the rocky portion of the property he tagged those wines "Gravelly Meadow."

Al's wines won acclaim. His insistence on the importance of the soil (the "terroir") gave impetus to a view of winemaking that was first fostered back in the 1890s by Gustav Niebaum, the Finnish sea captain who believed the soil itself and not just the winemaker's magic was the major factor in producing premium quality wines.

Like Niebaum, Al devoted much attention to his own personal setting, as well. With a garden featuring some 400 roses, plus azaleas, camellias, rhododendrons and nine waterfalls, his home has been the site of gatherings for the Jewish community, and he has contributed to the Napa Symphony, the Lincoln Theater, and the Parkinson Society.

Another Napa Valley vintner also had a French connection. Robert Mondavi had met Baron Philippe de Rothschild for the first time in Hawaii in 1970, and in the course of their evening together, the Baron casually proposed that the two might one day consider a joint venture. Eight years later Robert traveled to France to continue the conversation.

Baron Philippe was of the English branch of the Rothschild dynasty, his ancestor being Nathan, a London banker who had built himself a fortune through a shrewd understanding of how money works. Nathan became wealthy enough to supply cash for Wellington's army when they fought Napoleon at Waterloo. He invested in railroads and was banker to the likes of Metternich. One of his heirs, Nathaniel, purchased what was then Chateau Brane-Mouton in Pauillac in the Medoc region of France and renamed it Chateau Mouton-Rothschild.

Baron Philippe, Nathaniel's great-grandson, was a teenager during World War I. He spent the war at the winery, and in the Roaring Twenties he emerged to take on the Parisian social scene, which he did with gusto. He gained fame and mystique as a racecar driver, favoring Bugattis. He slipped away to North Africa during the Second World War, was arrested by the Vichy French, escaped and went to England; but his wife, Lilli, Countess de Chambure, was deported to the concentration camp at Ravensrueck, where she was murdered. Their daughter, Philippine, narrowly escaped the same fate. When the Germans came to arrest Lilli, the officer in charge spared the little girl because, he said, he had a child at home about her age.

After the war the grieving Philippe turned all his attention to the winery. Mouton-Rothschild had been a battlefield. Its vineyards were damaged and neglected, but the winemakers had been able to save some of the wines by walling them up within the facility. He gently nursed the winery back into operation. One of Baron Philippe's innovations—a strategy many have employed after his lead—was to commission famous artists to design his labels.

It was into this rich history that Robert Mondavi's winemaker son, Tim, stepped in 1979, when he and Mouton-Rothschild's Lucien Soinneau partnered to make a vintage together. The next year Robert and the Baron announced that the two wineries had established a 50-50 joint venture. The Mondavis sold thirty-five acres of their Napa Valley vineyard holdings to the partnership. The Mondavis and the Rothschilds selected an architect and began to build a winery: Opus One.

Unfortunately, Baron Philippe did not live to see the completion of the project. He passed away in 1988, but his daughter Philippine was on hand for the grand festivities when Opus One finally opened in 1991.

*   *   *

In the mid-1970s, America was hit with a recession. Free love, psychedelics and long gasoline lines contributed to a general feeling of unrest. Because of downturns in the economy, transitions in dress habits and problems within the extended family that comprised its upper management, Rough Rider closed its doors in 1977. Another Jewish-owned clothing manufacturer, Koret of California, bought Rough Rider's Oak Street facility for the preparation of ladies' slacks, which were then sent to San Francisco to be finished and pressed. Former Rough Rider executive Terry Savory managed the plant.

The image of a simple life in the Napa Valley with barrels of one's own vintage aging quietly in one's own winery was beginning to beckon, especially among the wealthy. There were times in his roller-coaster career when Leon Sange fit that description, and others when he definitely did not.[82] His grandfather was an intellectual and scholar who lived near the poverty level in Winnipeg after emigrating there from Russia. His grandmother probably worked. The oldest daughter moved to Oakland and started a chain migration of Sanges to California. To help with the family finances, Leon's father, Alexander, became a prizefighter for a while, an unlikely occupation for a Jew of his or any era. Eventually he owned a butter and egg company and married Irene Weinberg, daughter of a business colleague.

Leon inherited his grandfather's intellect and his father's competitiveness. After graduating from USC he earned a degree at Hastings School of Law in San Francisco. While he was still in grad school he met and married Nancy Noll, a Catholic, and upon graduation in 1969 landed a job at a prestigious law firm, where he did well right away.

His path, however, was not to be a smooth one. The day after the birth of Benjamin, their first child, Leon's boss fired him, leaving the family with no income. Leon moved his practice and brought most of his clients with him. In 1974 he entered a side business, buying a short-haul trucking company. The business worked out very well. He made money, and in 1976 he invested in a long-haul company. This time the plan backfired. Crippled with hidden debt from the outset due to faulty accounting practices, the long-haul enterprise folded.

The Sanges sold their large home in Piedmont and looked for a quiet country setting where they could raise their family while he concentrated on his law practice. Their quest brought them to St. Helena. They eventually purchased a ghost winery on Inglewood Avenue, with a vineyard planted in Green Hungarian grapes. They pulled out the Green Hungarian and planted Chardonnay, then rented the land to the Raymond Winery.

Leon was, in 1976, practically the only Jew in St. Helena. The Rosenbergers at Goodman's department store and Hanns Kornell also had St. Helena addresses, but none of them had children in the school system. Leon did not practice the faith, but he had by no means lost contact with the fact of his Jewish heritage. Others in the community also knew of his background. One day while waiting in line at the grocery store, Nancy heard a clerk say, "Don't worry; we know where all the Jews are, and we keep our eyes on them."

Before the decade was over, two Jewish brothers and their families had begun scoping out the prospects of moving to St. Helena's wine country. Alan, the older Finkelstein brother, was torn between following their grandfather's example and studying medicine, and becoming a professional musician. He changed his name to Alan Steen and worked his way through med school by playing the piano.

Alan was a surgical resident at LA County hospital and Art an architecture student at the University of Southern California when tragedy struck: Their father and their mother both passed away. Alan became the head of the family.

Alan and his wife Charlene, an attorney, became matchmakers. The pretty daughter of friends' friends, the Matzes, was attending rival UCLA. They arranged for Art to meet Bunnie Matz on Christmas Eve, 1964.[83]

Bunnie felt a certain comfort level with her date that night, a kind of coziness. It was mutual, and the warmth between them led to marriage in 1966.

In the early 1970s, after their son Judd was born, Art found himself drawn to the magic of winemaking. Their ancestors' cordial business was long gone, but Art and Alan had an urge to learn as much as they could about viticulture and enology, an interest that soon led them to Northern California, where they explored vineyards and sampled wines. One year Alan helped a vineyardist work the harvest and flew home on Southwest Airlines with 200 pounds of grapes stowed in plastic garbage bags and crammed in plastic containers. They did a cold fermentation in their garage.

It wasn't very good. Determined to do better, they contacted a home winemaking shop for advice and equipment. They began spending their weekends in Napa and Sonoma looking for property to buy. Alan kept Art supplied with grapes, and, with the help of the shop owner (John Daume) Art began to produce not just good wines, but award-winners. He won every amateur winemaking award around, with special kudos for his Chardonnays.

Bunnie, meanwhile, had gone back to school to become an ESL teacher. She was just starting her internship when the brothers found what they were looking for: centrally located acreage off of Whitehall Lane south of St. Helena, where the owner had a small (disease infested, as it turned out) vineyard and, even more important, a permit to build a winery. They bought it. While Bunnie continued with her teaching program, Art began to phase out his architecture firm, commuting every weekend to the Napa Valley. Alan and Charlene moved to a home on the property with their children, Eva, Larry and Sarah, and took enology courses at UC Davis.

The brothers sold their first crop to Charles Krug, then ripped out the existing vines and replanted with Cabernet, Merlot, Chardonnay and Chenin Blanc. Meanwhile, Art designed a new winery. They called it "Whitehall Lane" for the street near which it was located. Whitehall Lane Winery remained in the family from 1979 to 1988, growing from about 1,000 cases to 30,000.

Art and Bunny now have their own boutique winery, Judd's Hill, named for their son. Art designed the family's home around the winery, which is tucked away in the woodlands east of St. Helena.

The success of the Bernsteins, Brounsteins, Finkelsteins and Steens during the 1970s and early '80s encouraged others with equally small knowledge of the wine industry to trade in their three-piece suits for Levis.

The adventures of Jan Shrem are a case in point and a study in the unexpected. Jan was born in Colombia of Lebanese parents and moved to Jerusalem when he was two, then to New York. He worked as a messenger boy in the daytime and completed high school at night, receiving a scholarship to attend the University of Utah in the early 1950s. The heart of Mormon country was, indeed, a creative choice for a Jew. Gifted (or cursed) with an insatiable appetite for diverse experiences, he took what began as a short vacation in Japan while he was a graduate student at UCLA. The trip lasted thirteen years. He fell in love, and to support himself while courting his girlfriend Mitsuko, he started a business importing English-language reference and technical books.

It was a niche for which there was a huge market. He began translating and publishing books, as well, and by the time he eloped to Europe with Mitsuko he had created a publishing empire. He stayed in the business for a quarter century.

Mitsuko introduced Jan to wine and awoke in him a passion for the mysteries of the grape. In 1980 he enrolled in the University of Bordeaux to learn enology, a radical departure from his career as a publisher of technical books.

What particularly interested him also seemed incongruous: the combination of ancient winemaking practices with state-of-the-art technology. California was, he learned, revolutionizing the industry with new methodology and advanced equipment. The Napa Valley was the leader in this, so to the Napa Valley he went, stopping first, as Al Brounstein had done, at the office of Andre Tschelistcheff. Tschelistcheff became his advisor and close friend.

Jan bought fifty acres of vineyard in Calistoga in 1983 and added more as time went by. He sponsored an architects' competition to build a "temple to wine and art" that would showcase his impressive art collection, be a place of education and celebration, and at the same time be a working winery. Princeton architect Michael Graves won the contest and created Clos Pegase, which was completed in 1987.

The wine industry boomed in the 1980s, and not all the winery personnel who came to the Valley were neophytes. The family of

Michael Skalli had been in the business for three generations in France. The Skallis bought the old Dollarhide Ranch in Pope Valley in 1982, and in 1986 they purchased a high-visibility setting in Rutherford that once belonged to another French family, the St. Superys. St. Supery Winery debuted in 1990.

The Skalli family in Languedoc, France makes a kosher wine, Fortant de France. For a short time, St. Supery produced a kosher wine in Rutherford, Mount Madrona, (later called Mount Maroma) but production was complicated, there were lots of big competitors, and the market for it seemed small.

Not only that. As Nancy Noll Sange learned at the grocery store, reactionary elements still existed in the Napa Valley. A tough little courtroom pro was about to force a showdown with them that brought national attention to the quiet Napa Valley...

Chapter Twelve

In the days to come Jacob will take root,
Israel will bud and blossom
and fill all the world with fruit. —Isaiah 27:6

ELIZABETH ELLIS AND JEROME MAUTNER MET WHEN THEY WERE STU-
dents at Emory University in Georgia. Jerry's father had been a
Holocaust survivor; Elizabeth came from a long line of Methodist
ministers.[84] They were not a likely couple, but they enjoyed a
degree of simpatico that turned out to be the kind on which to build
a life together. They married.

After earning his law degree at Boston University, Jerry
accepted a job with the Department of Agriculture in New York
State, where he worked as an investigator. From there he moved to
the Department of Labor, where he began to gain impressive credentials as a crime fighter.

The couple lived in Mamaroneck, NY, in an apartment complex with many Jews. Elizabeth found herself drawn to Judaism not
only through Jerry, but through her friends there, as well. When a
gentile friend wanted to take lessons in Judaism through a local
Reform rabbi, Elizabeth came too and found herself persuaded. She
converted.

The health of the Mautners' oldest son, Michael, required that
the family move to a drier climate, so the Labor Department trans-

ferred the family to the West Coast. They found a home in Marin County. Within a year, though, Jerry began to long for more action. He took a position with an investigation firm back in New York. Elizabeth and the children (three of them by now) remained in Terra Linda to see if the new job was as good as it sounded before pulling up roots again.

It wasn't. Jerry returned to California with no job. His law credential wasn't valid in California, so he went to work for the Post Office and studied to take the California bar. When he passed it in 1973, the Solano County District Attorney's office hired him as a deputy DA.

The family needed a home closer to Jerry's new office, and they found the prices in nearby Napa to be affordably low, while the neighborhoods were pleasant and safe. They came to town on a Tuesday, and Friday night they attended Shabbat services at CBS, where they were enthusiastically greeted, especially, Elizabeth says, by the "wonderful, warm, inviting older members of the congregation." She remembers the women especially as being large-sized and always ready with a hug. It was a much-needed homey feeling for a transplanted easterner with four little boys at home.

What made the hominess even more complete was the presence of the Jewish community center with its centerpiece, the swimming pool. The uproar resulting from its creation had quieted down by now (although it wasn't completely forgotten), and the family spent their summers there, enjoying potlucks and warm relations with the rest of the congregation. Elizabeth taught Sunday School and served as the principal. A fifth son, John, was born.

Little by little, things began to change within the CBS community. The closure of Rough Rider had unexpected ramifications for the congregation. The merchandise that had lured so many people to the annual fund-raiser was no longer available; neither were the large donations from Rough Rider executives. It took a few years, but gradually CBS began to feel the pinch. Repairs and upgrades went by the wayside.

In the early 1980s an associate of Jerry's at the Solano DA's decided to run for District Attorney of Napa County against incumbent Jim Boitano. Jerry followed his associate's preliminary inquiries with much interest, as the police and sheriff's departments in Napa were seeking a more fervent crime-fighter than Boitano had been. What happened next raised Jerry's hackles. The Solano DA called Jerry's associate into his office and told him that if he ran against Boitano he'd be fired, but if he dropped out, he could become the chief deputy DA. Jerry learned that it was Boitano himself who had called his counterpart in Solano and manipulated the race.

His scruples deeply offended, Jerry decided to run for the post himself.

The congregation at CBS, whose philosophy was still to maintain a low profile and "not make waves," cringed at the thought of one of its members opposing District Attorney Boitano. Several members refused at first to support Jerry's campaign, and some who did asked that their names not be disclosed. When he won (by a huge margin of 66% to 34%), the members were generally restrained in their reaction, perhaps through disbelief. It was the most significant political victory for a Jew in the county's history.

He ran again, unopposed, in 1986.

Tough on crime and criminals, Jerry was hardly the type to not make waves; and in 1989 they came rolling in. A right-wing radical named Tom Metzger wanted to bring his "White Aryan Resistance" group to Napa County to recruit new members, and he planned the recruitment effort around a proposed rock concert which would feature several noted bands popular with "skinheads." It threatened to be a repeat of the enormous KKK convocations of the 1920s. The gathering would be on a field off Jamieson Canyon Road, a remote area in the southeast part of the county that was owned by a prominent right-wing physician from Vallejo, Howard Lonsdale; and it would be held on the Saturday that fifth son John Mautner was having his Bar Mitzvah.

Jerry was determined that no neo-fascist organization would be using Napa County as its stomping grounds and vowed to keep it out. What he encountered among his fellow administrators, however, was a low level of awareness about hate groups. The sheriff, for example, denied that white supremacist groups posed any problem for law enforcement. "They tend to draw organizations violently opposed to them and that tend [sic] to be the problem," the sheriff told the *Napa Register*. Such a problem group, he said, was the Jewish Defense League (JDL). "They do cause police problems."[85]

Jerry persisted. "I'd like to send out a message that this county is not a racist recruiting ground," he told the *Register*, adding that if the Board of Supervisors didn't want to get involved in the matter, he would file a suit himself: which he did.[86] He enjoined the Aryans from holding the concert on the technicality that they had not applied for a permit.

What was originally intended as an anti-black rally quickly became an anti-Semitic one. "No two-bit politician is going to do this to me," the *Register* reported Metzger as saying. The actual quote was, "No two-bit Jew..." While the crisis was on the way to its head, Debbie Norris (also Jewish), a secretary in Mautner's office, received an anonymous phone call saying, "Why are Jews allowed to have their Sunday Fun Day, when we can't have a concert?"

Bay Area Nazi organizer Bob Spittler seized on the controversy:

> Napa DA Jerome Mautner's pathetically
> transparent and hypocritical attempt to block
> our rock concert...is a text book illustration
> of this country's multiracial judicial system.[87]

The agency which the Aryans had approached to do the tick-

Napa Register, *3-18-1975*

Anne Percelay and daughter Debbie prepare for Passover.

*Larry Friedman didn't
mind poking fun at
himself. Many of his
Brewsters' ads show
him in caricature.*

From the Napa
Register, *date
unknown*

David Mendelsohn volunteered to service Israeli tanks in the 1980s.

Photo courtesy of Martha Pastcan

Left to right: Martha Pastcan, Susan Jacobs and Hanna Cassel at their B'not Mitzvah, December 15, 1984. It was the first time Congregation Beth Sholom allowed women on The Bima to read the Torah.

First confirmation at CBS. Left to right: George Rosenberg, confirmands Judd Finkelstein and Elizabeth Battat, and Rabbi David Kopstein. May 22, 1987.

George and Lottie Rosenberg helped found and lead Congregation Beth Sholom. Shown here in 1987.

Photo courtesy of Lottie Rosenberg

*Elizabeth and Jerry Mautner embrace their son John at
his Bar Mitzvah in 1989. Police stood guard outside.*

Robert Mondavi, Philippine and Baron Philippe de Rothschild

eting (BASS, a licensee of Ticket Master) happened to be owned by Bay Area Jews. They refused to have anything to do with the event.

The presence of "Aryans" and the Nazi party shivered the timbers of many a Napan. On the morning of the Board of Supervisors' meeting, 150 emotional spectators showed up, many of them Jewish, including Golden Lerman of Napa, who told the Aryans, "I grew up with the legacy that you people caused. I have no aunts and uncles." Choking back tears, she added, "I believe in the freedom of speech and the right to assemble, but not in the right to violence against minorities." Urging the supervisors to support Jerry's injunction, she concluded: "The eyes of the world are on us."[88]

It was true. Representatives from national magazines like *Newsweek* and the network media were circling Napa, hungry for soundbites.

Long dormant anger and resentment about the horrors of the Holocaust gnawed at the hearts of many in Congregation Beth Sholom. That night, "angry and frightened Napa residents" gathered at the Methodist church to organize their defense against the "Aryan Woodstock."[89]

Rabbi Trepp, identified by everyone except the Jews themselves as the local Jewish spokesman, said, "If we do nothing in the best of intent, it may be said of us in Napa that 'they didn't do anything.' That 'they didn't care'."[90] His reference, of course, was to those who knew of the Nazi horrors in Germany but never acted, like the rabbi who suggested he drown with the ship.

The next morning a panel of right-wing supporters and members of the gentile, Jewish, black and gay communities met together on a Bay Area TV talk show, among them Elizabeth Mautner. County Supervisor Mel Varrelman steered the course Jerry had mapped out: there would be no concert, he said, because the Aryans had failed to obtain a permit. Vitriolic exchanges among members of the panel (especially between the Jewish Defense League's Irv Rubin and the Aryans) revealed how close to the surface the currents of hate really were.

Napa's Jews held on tight and waited.

Meanwhile, the matter of the permit went to Superior Court Judge Scott Snowden for a ruling. With representatives of the Aryans, the JDL, the ACLU and a host of media reporters ready to pounce, Snowden dismissed Jerry's suit as "inflammatory" but then ruled on a similar suit brought by the county counsel in response to Jerry's efforts. Snowden agreed that the rally could go on but without music, due to the absence of the permit.

Saturday finally came; but the hordes of swastika-wielding Aryans for whom Metzger had hoped did not, nor did throngs of young people with shaved heads hoping to sign up. A heavy presence of law enforcement officers rimmed Lonsdale's field, which in itself may have been enough to discourage the thugs who might have attended. Metzger himself, it later turned out, was implicated in the murder of a black man.

In a way, the skinhead controversy helped to define where the Jews in Napa County stood in 1989. There was little support for right-wing hate groups, on the whole. It also became clear that Jews had some good friends in the community. The Family Support Network and the Methodist and Presbyterian churches were particularly vocal advocates, a mindset that continues to the present. The Napa Interfaith Council sponsors annual Holocaust Remembrance Day observances.

The Presbyterian pastor, Frank White, put an open invitation in the newspaper for all interested parties to come to CBS for John Mautner's Bar Mitzvah. Elizabeth feared that their son's very personal religious coming-of-age would turn into a psycho-socio-political disaster. This, too failed to materialize, and John's big day went off without a hitch, although the presence of armed police in and outside the synagogue spoke to many of the bad old days in countries far away.

Harry Martin, editor of the *Napa Sentinel*, used the incident as fodder for an on-going attack against the Mautners that he had begun in 1987. Some of his articles implied that the Mautner children were involved in drug abuse, an accusation that may have caused some in the congregation to shy away from the family.

One who never failed to express support for the Mautners was a young lawyer in the DA's office: Gary Lieberstein, a trim, friendly law-and-order advocate like Jerry. Gary would come to know first-hand the challenges of being District Attorney of Napa County.

Jerry ran again in 1990 and lost. Second son David, the Mautner child most frequently targeted by Martin, drowned in 1994. The Mautners were hurt by the failure of many at CBS to support the family during the *Sentinel's* tirades. After David's death they withdrew from the synagogue for a few years, until the wounds began to heal.

JDL firebrand Irv Rubin may have had more than one item on his agenda when he sat on the talk show panel that day in 1989. Rubin had an especially acute ear for hearing ethnic slurs, and thus was well suited in many ways to advocacy work. His father, an Orthodox Jew from Montreal, had shipped off to serve in the European Theater as a bombardier with the RCAF; Irv's mother drove an ambulance through the streets of London during the blitz. His maternal grandfather was deported to a Siberian gulag for activities against the Czar, and had he not jumped the train and found his way to Sweden (on foot) there would probably have been no Irv. Nor would there have been Irv's sister, Sandi, who, as Sandi Perlman had moved to Napa in 1973. Thus the other item on Rubin's agenda that day may have been to identify potential peril to his sister in the Napa Valley.[91]

Sandi Rubin Perlman opened the Napa Valley Emporium in 1979 to supplement the family's income while her husband Mike went back to school, and while for the most part she saw no evidence of discrimination, there was one nasty incident. In the mid 1980s a young man came into the store and wanted a cap with KKK printed on it. She told him she would not print that, and he insisted that she had to—she was being discriminatory. He became demanding, so she grabbed him by the scruff of his neck and made him leave the premises.

Sandi found that the local Jews had a very low profile and that the gentiles of the Napa Valley had minimal awareness of Judaism compared with people on the East Coast. After six months in her women's bridge club, for example, she informed her friends that she couldn't attend an up-coming meeting because of a Jewish holiday. The other members were shocked to learn she was Jewish.

While it was becoming safer to be a Jew in the Napa Valley, the skirmishes in Israel seemed endless. Around the same time as the skinhead controversy, future Napan David Mendelsohn, Deputy to the President of World Airways, felt moved to honor his ancestral identification with the embattled nation by helping to broker a deal between the Israeli government and the then Shah of Iran for planes and landing fields. Eager to do even more than he could accomplish in the boardroom, he also volunteered to assist the Israeli army by spending time at a military base there cleaning and repairing tanks.[92] During the 1980s and '90s quite a few congregants at CBS found time to go to Israel, some making the journey several times.

Jerry Mautner's terms as DA occurred at a time when other Jews were also finding their way into high-visibility positions in the community. Notable among them was former Rough Rider head Julian Weidler. Among his many accomplishments, Julian was President of the Napa Valley College Foundation and a founding member of the Napa Valley Economic Development Corporation. He brought S.C.O.R.E to Napa and volunteered there for a quarter century.

A trio of women also stood out as having made significant waves on the beachhead of social services.

Whitehall Lane Winery's Charlene Steen went back to school

and earned a Masters in Social Work and a PhD in Psychology to complement her law degree. Thus armed, she served as head of Sexual Assault Victims Services for Napa County and opened a private practice in Napa. Then she took a position as a correctional counselor/ psychologist at Vacaville Medical Facility in Solano County, where she stayed until 1992. She also found time to author material for professionals on the treatment of sexual offenders and their victims. She served on the boards of the Napa Valley Commission on the Status of Women (she was president for a term), the Napa Association for the Performing Arts, National Women's Political Caucus and If Given a Chance, along with some professional organizations.

Myrna Abramowicz's first job in Napa was as administrative assistant to Piercy Holliday, the Superintendent of Schools. It gave her a taste of politics that must have appealed to her very much, for she became a central figure in the local Democratic Party and in many community organizations throughout the '80s and '90s and into the present.

To name a few: Myrna was Napa County Chairperson for Alan Cranston and Barbara Boxer, on the executive board of the California Democratic Party and a delegate for Bill Clinton at the Democratic National Convention in 1992. She chaired the 8th Assembly District Caucus and the Napa Women's Political Caucus and served as campaign manager for several Napa County and City candidates. Governor Davis appointed her to the 25th Agricultural District Association, where she was vice president. She was secretary of the 1999-2000 Napa County Grand Jury and a trustee of Napa Valley Community College. The list of community organizations and causes she has supported is long, and she has not only made waves, she has induced a tidal surge in the service of social causes.Throughout all this, Myrna has been self-employed as a real estate broker.

Finally, there is Barbara Nemko, Napa County Superintendent of Schools.[93] As Barbara (Podridsky) Padrid, she grew up in the

Bronx and Flushing, Queens. When her father came with his family to Ellis Island from Poland as a child of eight, he was sequestered for some time due to a medical reason. It was terrifying, and while he never spoke of it, it hung over him for the rest of his life. Perhaps because of this, her first interest was in the humane treatment of children by public institutions. She became a school administrator.

Barbara came west to Berkeley in 1974. She was curious about the university's Advanced Reading Language Program, but fate (or God) had other plans. She and her then-boyfriend Marty Nemko attended a social event held by one of his colleagues. Unaware of the California custom of bringing a bottle of wine to a party, she brought the hostess a pie plate. This made a big impression on the woman, who forwarded to her the description of a new Master's Degree program, which she thought would fit the New York transplant. Barbara applied and was accepted and then transferred to a doctoral program, unaware that one doesn't usually "transfer" to a PhD program. She did it because it didn't occur to her that she couldn't.

After receiving her PhD in Education, she worked in the California Department of Education for twelve years, during which time she met Tony Apollini, Associate Superintendent at the Napa County Office of Education. He suggested she apply for the post of County Curriculum Director, which she did. It was hers. And when School Superintendent Ed Henderson ran for Mayor and won, she moved to Napa, applied for and received his vacated spot. She held the position for eighteen months, then ran for it in 1997 in a public election against an opponent with greater name recognition. She won again. She was re-elected in 2002.

Jewish women like Steen, Abramowicz and Nemko became, through their achievements, well-recognized throughout Napa County. Their religious orientation was moot; they were identified as assets to the community at large, not merely as representatives of a single faith.

Gary Lieberstein, elected District Attorney in 1998 and re-elected in 2002, has made the notion of community his philosophical centerpiece.[94] When the county was plagued with gang violence in the 1990s, he saw the problem as a matter affecting everybody. "This is everyone's community," he said. "This is not an Anglo or Latino problem, it is everyone's problem. I don't have a lot of patience for people who see such issues only in black, white or brown. We have to get beyond such thinking and work together as one."

Children, he believes, need to know they are part of the greater whole, and throughout his career he has sought ways to teach at-risk young people that opportunities for their betterment exist within the community. Much of his volunteer time is spent with organizations like the Child Abuse Prevention Council, If Given a Chance and the Napa County Juvenile Justice Planning Council.

Inclusive thinking such as that which Gary Lieberstein promotes is actually a new phenomenon in a region accustomed to cubby-holing ethnic issues. His warm reception with voters may be an indication that his viewpoint reflects that of many in Napa County. Be that as it may, some in the Jewish community still feel uncomfortable about making waves.

Chapter Thirteen

They shall build houses and dwell in them.
They shall plant vineyards and enjoy their fruit.
—Isaiah 65:21

CLAUDE ROUAS, THE RESTAURATEUR, REMAINED AT ERNIE'S RESTAU-
rant in San Francisco until 1966, when he opened his own very successful eatery, L'Etoile. He married again, and with his wife Ardath
had two daughters, Bettina and Claudia. On weekends the family
would escape to the Napa Valley. The trips became so frequent that
they bought a town house at the Silverado Country Club, which
became their base of weekend operations for a while.

By 1975 Claude was ready to consider putting up a small bed
and breakfast in the Valley and enhancing it with a first-class din-
ing room. He found a realtor who had, in fact, acquired a permit for
a hotel off the Silverado Trail in the hills southeast of St. Helena.
Once part of an olive grove, the land had dramatic views and was
relatively cheap: $125,000. They bought it.

Claude worked with San Francisco architect Sandy Walker and
interior designer Michael Taylor to develop plans for a restaurant
with overnight accommodations, but when they tried to interest
others in investing in the small resort, they were turned down. The

Napa Valley? Too remote. California wine? No future.

The only ally to fully appreciate Claude's vision was Robert Harmon, a developer associated with the Kaihuna Plantation in Kauai and Tahoe Tavern in the Sierras. In 1981, with Harmon as a partner, Claude opened a restaurant at the site of the little hotel he hoped to create. He would call the complex "Auberge du Soleil:" Inn of the Sun. He imported a high-priced New York chef, Masa, held his breath and opened for business.

Auberge du Soleil was a spectacular success. Diners soon had to make reservations months in advance. Herb Caen of the *San Francisco Chronicle* called it one of the best things to happen to the Napa Valley since Agostin Haraszthy arrived from Hungary to plant the first grapes.

Guests at Auberge often stayed for the entire weekend. To further accommodate them, Claude bought a run-down saloon in Yountville and converted it into an Italian restaurant he called "Piatti." It, too, was a success. In time he opened seventeen more Piatti restaurants, mostly in California but also in Texas, Washington, Portland and Denver.

Claude employed members of his family in his restaurants, giving them the experience they needed to make their own marks in the restaurant industry. His brother Albert became a familiar face at Piatti. His daughter Bettina furthered her education as a restaurateur with training in Paris and returned to the Napa Valley to become a manager at the French Laundry and then general manager at Bistro Jeanty and at Bistro Don Giovanni. In partnership with sister Claudia, Bettina now has her own restaurant in Napa's Hatt Building, "Angele's," named for Claude's mother.

Piatti and Auberge raised the ante for existing restaurants in the Napa Valley (there were few in 1981). More first-class eateries came with their top-notch chefs. The restaurants attracted tourists; the more tourists, the more new restaurants. Rouas' contribution to the Napa Valley was similar in some ways to that of the Jewish merchants a hundred years before him: the more stores, the more shoppers, the more shoppers, the more stores.

A corollary effect also occurred. The more good restaurants, the better the lifestyle, and the better the lifestyle, the higher the land values. The price of land in the Napa Valley rose phenomenally throughout the 1980s and '90s, especially from Yountville north, where most of the premium restaurants were located.

Among the world-class chefs to be attracted to the Napa Valley was Jan Birnbaum.[95] Jan was born in Baton Rouge, Louisiana, a busy southern city with a Jewish population big enough to support two synagogues. The whole family loved to cook, and although Jan got a degree in Petroleum Engineering from the University of Louisiana, after he graduated he chose to follow his genes and his bliss and found himself at K-Paul, the kitchen of famed Cajun restaurateur Paul Prudhomme. He learned the fundamentals of sound cooking. His rising career took him to the trendy and very pricey Quilted Giraffe in New York City, the equally upscale Rattlesnake Club in Denver, and then to elegant Campton Place in San Francisco, rated #1 by the *Conde Nast Traveler* and in the top ten by *Gourmet* magazine.

In 1994 he bought the restaurant and saloon at the Mt. View Hotel in Calistoga and created "Catahoula," which was the name of the Louisiana parish that hosted Baron de Hirsch's first agricultural settlement (see p. 54). The Catahoula is also the state dog of Louisiana (which is one reason many of Jan's friends in the business refer to him as "Big Dog"). Jan's cuisine combines the savory, spicy flavors of Cajun cooking with the zesty, fresh tastes of California cuisine.

Neither Claude Rouas nor Jan Birnbaum practices the faith, although both have strong Jewish identities. Each Passover, Jan offers a gourmet Seder, complete with cantor. He expected two dozen participants at the first and got a hundred.

Fully aware of the importance of wine to Jewish celebration, Napa's Ernie Weir bought 12+ acres of vineyard land off the

Silverado Trail in 1980, and while he continued to work for Domaine Chandon during the week, on the weekends he developed a vineyard and winery of his own. The result was Hagafen Cellars. (*Hagafen* is Hebrew for "the grapevine.") Hagafen produces Cabernet Sauvignon, Cabernet Franc, Pinot Noir, Merlot, Syrah, Chardonnay, Sauvignon Blanc, Johannisberg Reisling and a sparkling Brut Cuvee that won double gold medals at the California State Fair. The immaculate, compact winery building opened its doors in 2000. All of Ernie's wines are kosher.

A secular Jew, Ernie's Jewish identity is nevertheless very strong; indeed it is his taproot. He, wife Irit and their children (Maya, Jonathan and Tamar) have made numerous trips to Israel, including a year's sabbatical there in 2001, where he consulted for several Israeli wineries (among them Carmel, Yarden, Amphorae and Margalit).

Jewish identity is also a vital fact of life for the Bronfman family, whose connection to the Napa Valley began with Christian Brothers (if not secretly during Prohibition). Edgar Bronfman, heir to the Seagram's fortune, became president of the World Jewish Congress in 1981 and plied his considerable talent toward the project of unmasking former Nazis–he blew the whistle on Austria's Kurt Waldheim–and seeking reparations from the Swiss banking industry for hiding money believed to be stolen from Jews.

Samuel Bronfman II, is Chairman of Diageo Global Wines. Owned by Seagram's, Diageo produces and markets the wines of Sterling Vineyards and Beaulieu Viineyard.

The Up-Valley's reputation as a gastronomic Zion attracted the attention of a man who had made a fortune in the food and beverage industries: Leslie Gerald Rudd.

Leslie's father, Sam, graduated from the University of Denver in 1935 and started manufacturing wood cooperage for the Coors Bottling Company. When Kansas finally repealed its Prohibition laws in 1949, Sam moved the family to Wichita and sold cooperage there. He called his firm the Standard Mercantile Company, which morphed into the Standard Liquor Company and finally the Standard Beverage Corporation. It grew to become the biggest distributor of alcoholic beverages in Kansas.

Leslie attended the University of Wichita, and in 1965 he joined the company, eventually becoming president. On the side he also tinkered with some other enterprises. He was a founding partner in the Lonestar Steakhouse & Saloon (with franchises in Wichita and Charlotte, North Carolina) and a principal in Godfather Pizzas. In addition he owned several Pizza Hut franchises in the west and midwest. His endeavors made money.

In 1995 his private investment company, LRICo, bought controlling interest in a concern on the other end of the spectrum from the pizza business: Dean & Deluca, a fancy food emporium headquartered in Manhattan's SoHo district. The New York store—all 10,000 square feet of it—gained a reputation as a temple of culinary delights so alluring that it became a true Manhattan tourist attraction.

D&D now has stores in Washington, DC, Charlotte, Kansas City and in St. Helena.

The following year, he bought Girard, an Oakville-based winery and vineyard he renamed Rudd Vineyards & Winery. He replanted the vineyards, put in new tanks and expanded the existing 2,200 square feet of caves to 22,000 square feet.

His acquisitions extended beyond consumable products. Teaming with a friend, Todd Zapolski, he became a developer. In 1998 Zapolski + Rudd rehabilitated a Durham, North Carolina shopping center that was originally built in 1926. They turned it into a classy mall.

In 2002 Zapolski + Rudd bought Sawyer of Napa, part of the old Sawyer Tannery, which by then was no longer producing leather jackets or anything else. It had deteriorated into a low-rent warren of small businesses and light industries. Rudd was aware of the complex's historical value as well as its choice location on the Napa River. Refurbished and upgraded, Sawyer Tannery would be another money-winner.

Like most successful Jewish entrepreneurs, Leslie was moved to return a portion of his treasure to the greater community. In 1998 he established the Rudd Foundation, which engages in two very different endeavors. One is the Rudd Family Entrepreneurial Fund, which is open to students at all three public universities in Kansas. Students who would like to become entrepreneurs themselves are taught to submit business plans that are judged on their probability of success, student commitment and potential contribution to the community at large. The schools' Center of Entrepreneurship then provides professional advice regarding the plan and seed money— up to $250,000—to help get the young venture capitalists rolling.

The other is the Rudd Institute, which underwrites research to document, understand and reduce the stigma associated with obesity. Funded by the Rudd Institute, for example, researchers at Yale recently presented important data showing that the media portrays overweight people in negative roles, and that medical personnel and teachers often hold them in some disdain. Leslie became interested in obesity studies because he himself has been a victim of this modern epidemic.[96]

Locally, he gave at least $1.5 million to the Culinary Institute of America's Greystone facility to help create the Rudd Center for Professional Wine Studies, which among other things will provide two classrooms, each with a state-of-the-art "wine appreciation theater" designed to optimize the sensory evaluation of wine. Each student will have a personal light box for viewing the wine, an expectorant sink for tasting and a computerized means of tabulating their sensory findings. (Groundbreaking for the project was on March 13, 2003.)

Greystone, nee Greystone Cellars, is the enormous stone building just north of St. Helena that was once home to Christian Brothers Winery. CIA Greystone is the only facility in America devoted exclusively to the continuing education of personnel in the food, beverage and hospitality business.

Reuben Katz (no relation to Egon Katz) is CIA Greystone's Associate Managing Director.[97] He grew up in Pittsburgh, PA, in the heart of the Jewish enclave known as Squirrel Hill, once a hotbed of IWW anarchists (see p. 67). Reuben's mother died when he was very young, and his grandmother—a fabulous cook—raised him while his father worked in the fish business. His father's store was in the heart of Squirrel Hill, in an early supermarket that included a kosher butcher. The doorway between Katz's fish stall and Mr. Cohen's fresh-killed kosher poultry stall led to Mr. Adler's "appetizer" store, which sold all kinds of cheeses, smoked and cured products and canned and dry goods. A baker and a green-grocer held forth in adjacent stores. The market was alive with the sights and smells of a European *shtetl* and had a profound influence on young Reuben.

After graduating with a degree in Economics from the University of Pittsburgh (not surprising for a boy who grew up in the shadow of aging Bolsheviks), Reuben taught and then went into business, but the sensory allure of Squirrel Hill never left him. When he had amassed enough capital he returned to Pittsburgh and opened a restaurant, "La Normande." His first chef was a young man named Tim Ryan, who, as it turns out, is now President of CIA Greystone. One of his best customers was Ferdinand Metz, retired now but formerly the head of the Culinary Institute of America at its headquarters in Hyde Park, NY. Metz hired Tim Ryan away from Reuben.

Greystone's Rudd Center will give new life to Christian Brothers' old still house, a historically significant structure worth salvaging. After Leslie's seed money, others also contributed to the project, which is scheduled for completion in 2003.[98]

Luminaries like Rouas and Rudd have stunning records of achievement. The man whose life made the greatest impression on the Jewish community, however, was neither a connoisseur nor a titan of business. George Rosenberg, a man of simple tastes but boundless spiritual energy, guided Congregation Beth Sholom for forty-five years. When he passed away in 1998, his death left a vacuum. Several strong personalities emerged as potential leaders, but there was dissension regarding which direction the congregation now wanted to take and who would lead them. A number of members lobbied for moving away from the Conservative tradition and becoming a Reform synagogue.

After fifty years, CBS's physical plant was growing old. One of George's hopes had been that eventually the congregation would be able to replace its aging building with a more inspiring structure. As a tribute to their lost leader, the members voted to initiate a building campaign. At first the project galvanized the grieving Jewish community. People donated generously, especially in the first six months, which allowed the creation of preliminary feasibility studies.

A "Synagogue in the Vineyard" was envisioned. The project would include a Jewish cultural center that emphasized the Jews' ancient roots in winemaking and would appeal to Jews around the world—it would be a tourist destination in the heart of the wine country. Leslie Rudd offered a substantial donation to the project, provided that the other members also gave generously, as they were able.[99] The congregants held fundraisers toward the purchase of a suitable plot of land.

The building committee located several promising properties, among them a former strawberry field just north of Napa. In 2000, CBS member David Freed bought the "strawberry patch," and the committee investigated the concept of the congregation buying it from him and locating the synagogue there.

Jeff Morgan, a Jewish wine writer who at the time was wine director at Dean & Deluca, told the *San Francisco Chronicle* that

[i]t seems only natural that the 1000-plus Jews of

> Napa Valley should endeavor to create a Jewish
> cultural center and synagogue in the heart of
> America's premier wine region Many of us hope
> that such a center will serve as a bridge between
> Jews and non-Jews in the valley.[100]

The first big fundraising event was a lavish day-long tasting, dinner and auction with tours of Rudd Estate, Diamond Creek and Clos Pegase wineries, as well as contributions of vintages by Chameleon, Clos Pegase, Judd's Hill, Gelvani, Gemstone, Hagafen, Herzog, Richard Mendelson Winery and St. Supery. More than eighty people attended, and the effort netted about $12,000. It was an encouraging beginning.

But the "Synagogue in the Vineyard" was not to be, at least not just yet. Although sufficient funds were committed to secure the "strawberry patch," voices of caution spoke out. Some believed that the existing synagogue should simply be refurbished. Others warned that land-use issues in the county would propel the Jewish community onto the front pages of the local newspapers, attracting attention, making waves; and ultimately beckoning more Jews to a region that some still feared could turn coat on its Jewish citizens.

The plan fizzled. An anachronistic fear of anti-Semitism ruled the day.

Meanwhile, the members also sought to up-grade to a full-time, resident rabbi. Many were fond of their current rabbi, David White (who lived in Marin County) and wanted him to take the position, but White felt that his main gift was in facilitating small groups, not leading full congregations, and he did not want to leave Marin. His company, "Relationship Resources Unlimited," attracted a number of CBS congregants.

David Freed hired Rabbi White to be a "spiritual presence" for his vineyard investment company, UCC Vineyards, and that engagement evolved into WineSpirit, an "Institute for the Study of Wine and Spirituality," with the aim of helping people bring their spirituality to the secular world.

Perceiving a conflict of interest in Rabbi White's close working relationship with David Freed, several congregants pressed for terminating White's contract. Instead, members rose to praise White and offered him a salary hike. With the feisty Donna Heine in the lead, the discontented faction quit the synagogue soon after. Controversy over the rabbi and the failed building effort were not the only reasons for their departure. Although generally Conservative in style, Beth Sholom was not officially associated with any movement in Judaism. Heine and the other protesting members wanted to start a Reform synagogue. It represented more accurately, they believed, the inclinations of most Jews in Napa County and would draw in the unaffiliated. They incorporated as Congregation Emanu-el. Leslie Rudd assisted the new group with an anonymous financial contribution.

In 2003, the members of CBS also voted—overwhelmingly—to join the Reform movement. They then found a rabbi ordained in that tradition, James Brandt, a trained architect living in The Woodlands, a small community in Texas. Brandt agreed to move to the Napa Valley and become CBS' first full-time resident rabbi. Rabbi White went on a month-to-month contract and continued his small groups, while the congregation awaited the arrival of their new leader. The Napa Valley now had two Reform congregations, both in the city of Napa.

Chapter Fourteen

Watch over this vine,
The root your right hand has planted,
The branch you have raised up for yourself.
—Psalm 80:15-16

The Jews who have come to live in the Napa Valley at the turn of the new century find themselves in a place that in some ways never quite left the 1960s. The community at large has an old-fashioned feel to it. Not really urban, many gentiles in Napa County "don't know from Jewish," as CBS lay leader Art Finkelstein once put it. The membership fee at the synagogue—$600 per family in 2002— was by far the lowest in Northern California.

It is a 1960s without the dark side. The bane of anti-Semitism appears to be quiet in the Napa Valley now, despite the fears of some at CBS. Former St. Helena merchant Ada Press, who came to the Valley in 1993, says she never experienced discrimination during her eight-and-half years with On the Vine.[101] With Leon Sange's Napa Valley Coffee Roasting Company around the corner, hers was not the only Jewish-owned enterprise there: another positive sign.[102]

Mautner family foe Harry Martin of *The Sentinel* was re-elected to the Napa city council in 2003. Sharing the table with him this time, however, is the first Jew to be elected to that body—Dr. Lee Block's son, Kevin. Ethnicity appears immaterial to most gentiles. The toughest overt problems facing local Jews who worship regularly may be those related to their own self-governing and their fear of the re-emergence of ethnic hatred.

The reorganization of the Jewish community into two separate congregations has come at a time when American Jews in general are moving away from moderate branches of Judaism. More Jews than ever before are identifying themselves as secular, while at the same time Orthodox and ultra-Orthodox congregations experience growing memberships with younger congregants. It is a trend shared by mainstream Protestant churches. Charismatic and evangelical groups like the Mormons and Assemblies of God report double-digit growth, while Episcopalians and Presbyterians, for example, have lost members.[103]

One reason for the diminishing numbers among Reform and Conservative Jewish congregations is that many couples are starting later to have smaller families:

> Fifty two percent of Jewish women ages 30-34
> have no children, compared to 27 percent of
> all American women. Reserchers found that
> Jewish women who are approaching the end
> of the childbearing years have had approximately
> 1.8 children, [which] is below the replacement level
> of 2.1, contributing to the downward trend in the
> population. [104]

Extended schooling, increased vocational opportunities for women and heightened social consciousness concerning issues of over-population are cited as among the reasons for this apparent decline. Orthodox and ultra-Orthodox Jewish women (as well as

socially conservative gentiles) continue to have larger families earlier.

Some have speculated that the real culprit behind the drop in
synagogue attendance is an apparent paradox: With the decline of
scapegoating and persecution, they say, Judaism is seen as nothing
special. Many Jews are asking, Why be Jewish? Like the Sephardic
and Ashkenazi immigrants who trickled in prior to 1848, many
Jews have simply become assimilated into the dominant culture
and no longer identify themselves as Jewish. Their children and
grandchildren stand to lose any knowledge of their forebears' spiritual orientation and ethnic legacy.

More Jews marry outside the faith today, and the stigma for
doing so is considerably less.[105] This statistic is especially trou-
bling to those (usually Orthodox) who believe that intermarriage
with non-Jews inevitably results in loss of Jewish identity.

> Demographers predict an American Jewish
> community one-third to one-sixth its current
> size within two generations. Already 70,000
> more children under the age of 9 are being
> raised in homes with one Jewish parent than
> are being raised in homes with two Jewish parents.
> Being raised in such a one-Jewish-parent home
> virtually guarantees the child's loss to the
> Jewish community. [106]

Be that as it may, every person interviewed for this book—
even the most secular—described him- or herself as definitely
"feeling" Jewish.

Approximately 127,000 people lived in Napa County in 2000.
There were estimated to be about 1,400 Jews in the area, or about
1% of the total population. For a rural location, this is a surprisingly high ratio. Relatively few Jews, however, make the synagogue
the focal point of their lives. There were only 164 active membership units before the schism of 2001 and far fewer in splinter

Congregation Emanu-el.

A large proportion of the Napa Valley's Jews, like Julian Weidler, Barbara Nemko and Gary Lieberstein, express their Jewish values in their personal involvement within the community—whatever they see their community to be. Members of the Jewish Historical Society of the Napa Valley, which the Mendelsohns and Zoe and Howard Kahn began in 2002, gather to explore their personal ancestry. The Jewish Community of the Napa Valley, established in 1998 under the directorship of Dr. Alvin "Lee" Block, is a group of local Jewish philanthropists who find worthy charitable or cultural causes to support financially. The group only funds two or three projects per year, so the donation makes a sizeable difference.

Others engage in outreach abroad. Gene (Egon) Katz was instrumental in helping his hometown of Barntrup, Germany erect a memorial to the victims of Nazi persecution. David Mendelsohn is a regional representative for AIPAC, the American-Israel Public Affairs Committee, an important Washington, DC lobby. When Ernie and Irit Weir go to Israel, they engage in "Living Room Dialogues" that bring Muslim and Jew together in a mutual and personal search for common ground. They hope to establish a sister-city-type relationship between the Israeli wine country around Binyamini and Zichron Yaakov, and the Napa Valley.

Today's Napa Valley Jews are not primarily merchants; many are connected to the wine business as growers, vintners, managers, wine writers, etc. Others are in the arts, like musician Marcia Battat and noted Napa Valley Symphony conductor Asher Raboy. Carolyn Bloom, wife of PR specialist Harvey Posert, was a PR specialist herself before moving to St. Helena, and before that a performer with New York's "Best of Broadway." She has sung services at many prominent synagogues on the East Coast. Helene Glickfeld Marshall is an artisan whose work once drew the attention of Martha Stewart; she and her husband are also bee-keepers with an apiary in American Canyon.[107]

As described in the foregoing, Jews played an important role in the founding of the communities of the Napa Valley. Their departure around the time of the First World War represented, in large part, a reaction to the narrowing of perspective experienced in many American rural communities. This xenophobia persisted through the Second World War and continued in the cities of Napa County almost into the present. The Jews who made the Valley their home during this time kept, for the most part, a low profile, fearing to "make waves" and arouse anti-Semitism. Newcomers who threatened this position sometimes met hostility from other Jews, and anxiety about rekindling further anti-Semitism still exists within the Jewish community.

After the skinhead showdown of 1989 and the high-visibility success of Jews in prestigious venues—particularly the wine and food industry—most have come to challenge the "don't make waves" admonition. Jews now serve as community leaders and role models, and their numbers here are once again on the rise.

God's ancient promise of peace under the vine and the fig tree may at last be fulfilled, at least in the Napa Valley.

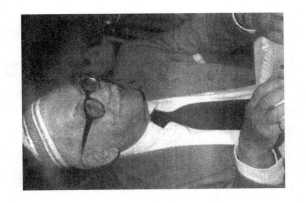

Left, Rabbi David White, and above, Rabbi George Vida.

Zoltan and Sara Rosenberger in 2003.

Wine men: Al Brounstein (seated) with Jan Shrem (left) and Leslie Rudd at a CBS fund-raiser in the caves at Shrem's Clos Pegase Winery.

Renaissance couple: Art and Bunnie Finkelstein are artists (some of Bunnie's work is shown here) and musicians (she plays tuba, he plays piano). Art is lay leader at CBS, and Bunnie supervises Oneg Shabat.

Napa Valley restaurateur Jan Birnbaum

תשייס

Photo courtesy of Dona Kopol Bonick

Ernie Weir of Hagafen Winery

Photo courtesy of Claude Rouas

Founder of Auberge du Soleil and Piatti, Claude Rouas raised the ante for area restaurateurs.

Photo courtesy of CIA Greystone

Reuben Katz

Photo courtesy of Dona Kopol Bonick

Sam Bronfman II

Popular DA Gary Lieberstein in April, 2003

*No longer dancing, Roz Johnson (seated) enjoys
a hug from fellow congregant Ada Press.*

Congregation Beth Sholom, 2003

Notes for Part One

Chapter One

1. For a thorough history of the Jews in Europe, see Solomon Grayzel, *A History of the Jews*, The Jewish Publication Society of America, Philadelphia, 1960.

2. Ibid, p. 295.

3. Idem.

4. Ibid, p. 308.

5. Miriam Weinstein, *Yiddish: A Nation of Words*, Steerforth Press, S. Royalton, NJ, 2001, p. 15.

6. Grayzel, Op. Cit., pp. 312-313.

7. Museum Judengasse, *www.judengasse.de.*

8. Niall Ferguson, *The House of Rothschilld: Money's Prophets, 1798-1848*, Penguin Books, New York, NY, 1999, p.3.

9. Weinstein, Op. Cit., p. 16.

10. Grayzel, Op. Cit., p. 447.

11. Weinstein, Op. Cit., p.26.

12. Rabbi Ken Spiro, "Crash Course in Jewish History," Part 48, *www.aish.com*, p. 4.

13. Rabbi Lee J. Levenger, PhD, *A History of the Jews in the United States*, Union of Hebrew Congregations, New York, 1967, p. 35.

14. Grayzel, Op. Cit., pp. 323-325.

15. Spiro, Loc. Cit.

16. Grayzel, Op.Cit., pp. 502-503.

17. Levenger, Op. Cit., p. 124.

18. Stanley Feldstein, *The Land That I Show You*, Anchor Books, Garden City, NY, 1979, p. 62.

19. According to Levenger (Op. Cit., p. 177) the new round of anti-Semitic persecutions was the most severe in Bavaria, which consequently had the greatest number of emigrants. Immigration records of many Napa County Jews report Bavaria as the site of their birth.

Chapter Two

20. Claire Erks, interview with author, 9-23-2002.

21. Campbell Menefee, *Historical and Descriptive Sketch Book of Napa, Solano, and Lake Counties, 1873,* James D. Stevenson, Fairfield, CA, 1993, p. 22.

22. Ibid, p. 21.

23. *St. Helena Star (SHS)*, 10-2-1874.

24. Robert E. Levinson, *The Jews in the California Gold Rush,* Judah L. Magnes Museum, Berkeley, pp. 73-74.

25. *Napa County Reporter (NCR)*, 8-4-1866.

26. Menefee, Op. Cit., p. 57.

Chapter Three

27. Many of the Sephardic Jews were wealthy and had come to America (and subsequently California) to seek new markets. See Levinger, p. 11.)

28. At least one Level may have stayed behind. A "Guillaume Levels" (sic) married Rudolph Baum in San Francisco in 1885 and may have been related.

29. Lyman Palmer, *History of Napa County*, Slocum & Bowen, San Francisco, 1881, p. 517

30. Many Sephardic Jews emigrated to the American south. See Fred Rosenbaum, *Visions of Reform: Congregation Emanu-el and the Jews of San Francisco,* Judah L. Magnes Museum, Berkeley, 2000, p. 2.

31. A section of it, as quoted in Levinger, Op. Cit., p. 75.:

> What prayers were in this temple offered up
>> Wrung from sad hearts that knew no joy on earth,
> By these lone exiles of a thousand years,
>> From the fair sunrise that gave them birth

32. Ibid, p. 58.

33. Harriet and Fred Rocklin, *Pioneer Jews: A New Light in the Far West,* First Mariner Books, New York, 2000, p. 26.

34. Palmer, Op. Cit., p. 567.

35. Janett may have been related in some way to Daniel Levy of Lorraine, who arrived in San Francisco in 1855 and taught in Rabbi Elkan Cohn's religious school there.

36. Palmer, Op. Cit., p. 343. J.N. Faulkenstein was a charter member of the United Workmen, too. A. Korns, likely also Jewish, was among the first to join the Odd Fellows.

37. Bloch's ads were especially aggressive. One in the *Napa Reporter* (12-15-1882) urged shoppers to try his store first, because "He Means Business!" and his merchandise was at "bedrock prices."

38. Alden had been a partner at Levinson's.

39. *SHS,* 7-27-1877.

40. *SHS,* 1-24-1879

41. *SHS,* 8-3-1945.

42. Prominent Napa bankers James and George Goodman, no relation to Abraham Goodman, were born in Rochester, NY to Harvey and Mary Negus Goodman. Robert E. Levinson, author of *Jews in the California Gold Rush* and

the late local historian D.T. Davis both identified the Goodmans as Jewish. After their parents' death the Goodman brothers lived for a time in Memphis, where there were other Goodmans and a large Jewish population. They came to San Francisco in 1852 and set up a merchandising business on Front Street, and later similar stores in Napa and Nevada City. The Napa Goodmans did not practice Judaism. If their father Harvey was, indeed, ethnically Jewish, he was in all probability assimilated, a common fate for Jews who came to America before 1848.

43. Nathan Lauter's granddaughter, Marge, married William Zellerbach.

44. *SHS*, 4-27-1900. Which Levy brothers they were is open to conjecture, although both E.J. Levy and M.S. Levy lived in St. Helena when Lauter did.

Chapter Four

45. *Calistoga Tribune*, 6-9-1872.

46. Palmer, Op. Cit., p. 464.

47. *Calistoga Tribune*, 1-4-1872

48. Palmer, Op. Cit., p. 177.

49. Robert Louis Stevenson, *Travels With a Donkey; An Internal Voyage; The Silverado Squatters*, ed. by Trevor Royle, J.M. Dent, Rutland, VT, 1993, p. 240.

50. Ibid, pp. 249-250.

51. *SHS*, 2-23-1877.

52. *SHS*, 10-20-1876.

Chapter Five

53. Claire Erks, interview with author, 9-23-2002.

54. At least for some. Within Judaism there is also a strong iconoclastic tendency that values independent thinking and discourages blind acceptance of group norms.

55. An ad in 1896 announced a "sensation in trowsers" at Alden & Levinson.

56. *Napa County Reporter (NCR)*, 2-23-1861.

57. Louis Ezettie, *Napa Register (NR)*, 11-28-1962.

58. It's now the site of a parking lot.

59. *NJ*, 2-9-1936.

60.The store closed in 1953 and burned down in 1962.

61. *NDJ*, 7-9-1932. The Weils were influential merchandisers.

62. *Napa Weekly Recorder*, 7-14-1890.

63. *NDJ*, 6-18-1890.

64. Steve Gordon, interview with author, 10-1-2002.

65. *NDJ*, 12-12-1900.
66. *NCR*, 12-1-1882.
67. *NJ*, 5-27-1892.
68. *NDJ*, 2-16-1901.
69. "The Story of Napa Leather," unpublished manuscript, Sawyer Tannery, 1944 and 1946.
70. Ada F. Kahn, *Jewish Voices of the California Gold Rush*, Wayne State University Press, Detroit, 2002, pp. 278-281.
71. Palmer, Op. Cit., p. 517.
72. William Heintz, *California's Napa Valley: One Hundred Sixty Years of Winemaking*, Scottwall Associates, SF, 1999, p. 123.
73. Ibid, p. 144.
74. *SHS*, 10-7-1892.
75. Palmer, Op. Cit., p. 585.
76. *SHS* , 4-21-1882.
77. Palmer. Op. Cit., p. 219.
78. Heitz, Op. Cit., p. 131.
79. *SHS*, 3-24-1882.

Chapter Six
80. Grayzel, Op. Cit., p. 638. Grayzel says that the pogroms were stimulated by Christian merchants who competed with the Jews commercially.
81. Ibid, p. 639.
82. Ibid, p. 657.
83. Ibid, p. 660.
84. Jack Glazier, *Dispersing the Ghetto*, Cornell University Press, Ithaca, 1998, pp. 38-39.
85. Art and Bunnie Finklestein, interview with author, 2-3-2003.
86. Alan and Charlene Steen, interview with Sonya Milton, 1-29-2003.
87. *http://collections.ic.gc.ca*
88. Rozaline Johnson, interview with author, 8-19-2002.
89. Ellie Meyer, interview with Sonya Milton, 9-17-2002.
90. Heitz, Op. Cit., p. 142.
91. Ibid, p. 119.
92. California Wine Association records, *http://findaid.oac.cdlib.org*.
93. See Charles Sullivan, *Napa Wine: A History*, Wine Appreciation Guild, SF, 1994, p. 119.

Notes for Part Two

Chapter Seven

1. *NDJ,* 1-6-1916.
2. *NDJ,* 4-4-1918. That Grauss was Jewish is probable.
3. *NDJ,* 4-21-1918. Some or all of the trio may have been Jewish.
4. *NDJ,* 10-15-1918.
5. Martin Gilbert, *The First World War: A Complete History*, Henry Holt and Company, NY, 1994, p. 103.
6. See Kenneth L. Kann, *Comrades and Chicken Ranchers: The Story of a California Jewish Community*, Cornell University Press, Ithaca, 1993.
7. Levinger, Op. Cit., p. 496.
8. The demand for quicksilver declined with the end of the Gold Rush.
9. *SHS*, 6-29-1917.
10. *NDJ*, 5-4-1918.
11. *NDJ*, 4-27-1918.
12. Levinger, Op. Cit., pp.291-2. See also "Zionism: The National Liberation Movement of the Jewish People," by Professor Robert Rockaway, at *www.azm.org/essays/rockaway/.html*
13. Weinstein, Op. Cit., p. 74.
14. The League of Nations held the knife, but the major powers told it where to cut.
15. Zoltan and Sara Rosenberger, interview with the author, 10-6-2002.
16. *SHS,* 10-26-1923
17. *SHS*, 8-8-1924.
18. *SHS,* 4-11-1924.
19. *SHS*, 8-5-1904.
20. *SHS*, 11-4-1904.
21. Carole Hicke, "Diamond Creek Vineyards: The Significance of Terroir in the Vineyard," Regents of the University of California, Berkeley, 2000, p. 1.
22. George Altamura, interview with the author, 1-29-2003. Over time Sam acquired quite a lot of land in the Napa area, including a large piece just south of what is now Old Sonoma Road. There, during the World War II housing boom, he built a housing development and a "modern" shopping mall with Food City as its central attraction. Sam was known for his honesty and integrity, and thus was easy to do business with. He was not religious, but when he died in 1971, Dr. Morris Goldstein of Sherith Israel conducted the funeral. (*NR*, 5-10-1971)
23. now University of the Pacific
24. Ellie Meyer, interview with Sonya Milton, 9-17-2002.

Final

Chapter Eight

25. *SHS*, 4-27-1934.

26. specially trained worker who observes kosher laws

27. *SHS*, 8-10-1934.

28. *NJ*, 8-18-1935.

29. Augmenting the Ivy League's anti-Semitism was the publication of certain pseudoscientific works in psychometrics and sociology with racist premises. See Stephen Jay Gould, *The Mismeasure of Man*, W.W. Norton, New York, 1981.

30. *NR*, 1-7-1963.

31. *NJ*, 7-7-1935.

32. Interview, 1-29-2003.

33. See Jack Glazier, *Dispersing the Ghetto: The Relocation of Jewish Immigrants across America*, Cornell University Press, Ithaca, NY, 1998.

34. *NJ*, 2-14-1936.

35. As early as 1922, a Napa newspaper reported that the Nazi party planned to boycott the businesses run by German Jews—*NJ* 3-28-22.

36. Egon and Elisabeth Katz, interview with Sonya Milton, 1-7-2003.

37. Richard D. Bank, *Why Be Jewish?* Jason Aronson, Inc., Northvale, NJ, 2001. Some estimates ran as high as 1100 synagogues burned and 300 people killed.

38. Rabbi Leo Trepp, interview with Sonya Milton, 2-13-2003.

39. Marilouise Kornell, interview with the author, 12-16-2002.

40. As late as 1939 the Nazis were still releasing some of the Jews they had imprisoned, contenting themselves with merely causing them pain and suffering. Eichmann's hideous "final solution" plan began later.

41. Ruth Teiser, "Alfred Fromm: Marketing Wine and Brandy," The Regents of the University of California, Berkeley, 1984, p. 10.

42. Dilys Jones, *San Francisco Chronicle*, 6-8-1953.

43. *Jewish Bulletin of Northern California*, 7-10-1998.

44. Grayzel, Op. Cit., p. 784.

45. Henry Michalski, interview with Sonya Milton, 2-20-2003.

46. J.J. Goldberg, *Jewish Power: Inside the the American Jewish Establishment,* Addison-Wesley Publishing Company, Inc., Reading, MA, 1996, p. 115.

47. See Peter Novick, *The Holocaust in American Life*, First Mariner Books, Boston, 1999.

48. Anecdote courtesy of *Napa Register* newspaper columnist Yvonne Baginsky, who interviewed Karola near the end of her life. Polish Catholics

also saw the inside of Hitler's concentration camps. Baginsky's parents were among them.
49. Grayzel, Op. Cit., 788.

Chapter Nine
50. Lottie Rosenberg, interview with Sonya Milton, 9-17-2002.
51. Their endeavor had no connection with the chicken farmers in Petaluma.
52. *NCR,* 6-22-89.
53. Idem.
54. Harry's daughter married Mervyn Morris, founder of Mervyn's Department Store, and Albert's became one of the first in that chain.
55. *NCR,* 6-22-1989.
56. Grayzel, Op. Cit., p. 809.
57. B'nai B'rith began in 1843 as a secret fraternal order, like the Masons, but soon dropped its mysticism in favor of providing practical help and social and cultural opportunities for Jewish men. Also like the Masons, it has chapters worldwide.
58. Novick, Op. Cit., p. 83.
59. Claude Rouas and Alexandrine Venezia, interview with Sonya Milton, 2-12-2003.
60. Sullivan, Op. Cit., p. 247.
61. Julian Weidler, interview with Sonya Milton, 1-12-2002.
62. Alice Cohen-Peterson, interview with Sonya Milton, 11-23-2002.
63. the oldest of whom, Charles, became an English professor at Berkeley, holding the Chaucer Chair for Literature.

Chapter Ten
64. Myrna Abramowicz, interview with Sonya Milton, 1-8-2003.
65. Larry and Rachel Friedman, interview with Sonya Milton, 10-17-2002.
66. Terri Linn, interview with Sonya Milton, 11-20-2002.
67. *NR,* 11-30-1962.
68. Anne Percelay, interview with Sonya Milton, 2-15-2003.
69. Donna Heine, interview with Sonya Milton, 12-6-2002.
70. They were: Rabbis George Vida, David Kopstein, Samuel Broude and David White.
71. Alvin Lee Block, MD, interview with Sonya Milton, 1-28-2003.
72. Quite a few excellent Jewish physicians have found their way to Napa. Among them are dermatologist Diane Silver and her brother Jerome Soloman, an OB-GYN; vascular surgeon Richard Bien, whose mother Karola's story is

recounted elsewhere in this book; Kaiser Permanente physicians Richard Pastcan and Richard Lenson, who are both active at CBS; psychiatrists Eliot Percelay and Howard Eisenstark and psychologist Leo Stoer; rehabilitation specialist Corby Kessler; and allergist Larry Posner. There are others, as well.

73. It later became Buchanan's stationery store.

74. Harvey Posert and Carolyn Bloom, interview with the author, 12-31-2003.

75. The Valley, in turn, has embraced Harvey. His PR acumen helped the Robert Mondavi Winery reach the pinnacle of success in the industry, and many an entrepreneur has benefited from his wisdom as a consultant.

76. "Alfred Fromm: Wines, Music and Lifelong Education," Interview by Elaine Dorfman and Caroline Crawford, 1986, 87. Community Oral History Project, Bancroft Library, Berkeley, CA.

77. John Koopman, *SF Chronicle*, 1-11-2003.

78. Arlene Bernstein, personal correspondence with the author, 2-17-2003.

Chapter Eleven

79. Albert Brounstein, "Diamond Creek Vineyards: The Significance of Terroir in the Vineyard," interview by Carole Hicke, The Regents of the University of California, Berkeley, 1998, p 12.

80. Ibid, p. 23.

81. Ernie Weir, interview with the author, 2-20-2003.

82. Nancy Haynes, interview with the author, 2-17-2003.

83. Art and Bunnie Finkelstein, interview with the author, 2-3-2003.

Chapter Twelve

84. Jerry and Elizabeth Mautner, interview with the author, 2-3-2003.

85. *NR*, 2-24-1989.

86. *NR*, 2-25-1989.

87. *NR*, 3-1-1989.

88. *NR*, 2-28-1989.

89. *NR*, 3-1-1989.

90. Idem.

91. Sandi Perlman, interview with Sonya Milton, 2-6-2003.

92. Donna Mendelsohn has also donated time and treasure to the young country. During a peaceful lull, she brought twenty-two Girl Scouts (Jew and gentile) to Israel and spent six weeks there touring, camping, and meeting with other Scouts. Afterward, she was instrumental in bringing Israeli scouts to America to enjoy similar adventures.

93. Barbara Nemko, interview with Sonya Milton, 2-12-2003.

94. Gary Lieberstein, interview with the author,, 3-5-2003.

Chapter Thirteen
95. Jan Birnbaum, interview with the author, 1-31-2003.
96. Karen N. Peart, Yale University, *karen.peart@yale.edu.*
97. Reuben Katz, interview with the author, 3-13-2003.
98. Including the Napa Valley Vintner's Association, Viking Range, and individual participants like the Cakebread family, Joel Peterson and Reed Foster.
99. Jim Heaphy, interview, 2-24-2003
100. *SF Chronicle*, 9-21-2001.

Chapter Fourteen
101. Ada Press, interview with Sonya Milton, 2-5-2003.
102. CBS member Bunny Goldstein once quipped that "two more Jews in St. Helena and the Jewish population goes up 50%."
103. *www.washington post.com*
104. *www.tdhs-nw.org*
105. Alan M.Dershowitz, *The Vanishing American Jew*, Little, Brown & Company, Boston, 1997, p. 28.
106. Jonathan Rosenblum, "Get Me to the Church on Time," *Jerusalem Post* International Edition, 1-5-2001.
107. Helene Marshall, interview with Sonya Milton, 3-29-2003.

Bibliography

Bank, Richard D. *Why Be Jewish?* Northvale, NJ: Jason Aronson, Inc., 2001.

Bard, Mitchhell G. *Myths and facts: A Guide to the Arab-Insraeli Conflict.*
Chevy Chase, MD: American-Israeli Cooperative Enterprise, 2001.

Bower, Tom. *Nazi Gold.* NY: HarperCollins, 1997.

Corosso, Vincent. *The California Wine Industry, 1830-1895.* Berkeley:
University of California Press, 1951.

Dershowitz, Alan M. *The Vanishing American Jew.* Boston: Little, Brown &
Company, 1997.

Falcon, Rabbi Ted. *Judaism for Dummies.* NY: Hungry Minds, Inc.,2001.

Feldstein, Stanley. *The Land That I Show You.* Garden City, NY: Anchor
Books, 1979.

Ferguson, Niall. *The House of Rothschilld: Money's Prophets, 1798-1848,*
NY: Penguin Books, 1999.

Ferguson, Niall. *The House of Rothschild: The World's Banker, 1849-1999.*
NY: Penguin Books, 2000.

Fradkin, Philip. *Stagecoach.* NY: Simon & Schuster Source, 2002.

Gilbert, Martin. *The First World War: A Complete History.* NY: Henry Holt
and Company, 1994.

Glazier, Jack. *Dispersing the Ghetto: The Relocation of Jewish Immigrants
Across America.* Ithaca, NY: Cornell University Press, 1998.

Goldberg, J.J. *Jewish Power: Inside the the American Jewish Establishment,*
Reading, MA: Addison-Wesley Publishing Company, Inc., 1996

Gould, Stephen Jay. *The Mismeasure of Man.* NY: W.W. Norton, 1981.

Grayzel, Solomon. *A History of the Jews.* Philadelphia: The Jewish Publication
Society of America, , 1960.

Heilman, Samuel C. *Portrait of American Jews: The Last Half of the Twentieth
Century.* Seattle: University of Washiington Press, 1998.

Heintz, William. *California's Napa Valley: One Hundred Sixty Years of
Winemaking.* SF: Scottwall Associates, 1999.

Kahn, Ada F. *Jewish Voices of the California Gold Rush.* Detroit: Wayne State
University Press, 2002.

Kann, Kenneth L. *Comrades and Chicken Ranchers: The Story of a California Jewish Community.* Ithaca, NY: Cornell University Press, 1993.

Levenger, Rabbi Lee J. , PhD. *A History of the Jews in the United States.* NY: Union of Hebrew Congregations, 1967.

Levin, Marlin. *It Takes a Dream: The Story of Hadassah.* NY: Gefen Books, 1997.

Levinson, Robert E. *The Jews in the California Gold Rush..* Berkeley: Judah L. Magnes Museum, 1978.

Menefee, Campbell. *Historical and Descriptive Sketch Book of Napa, Solano, and Lake Counties, 1873.* Fairfield, CA: James D. Stevenson, 1993.

Meyer, Martin, ed. *Western Jewry.* SF: Emanu-el, June, 1916.

Novick, Peter. *The Holocaust in American Life.* Boston: First Mariner Books, 1999.

Palmer, Lyman. *History of Napa County.* San Francisco: Slocum & Bowen, 1881.

Rochlin, Harriet and Fred. *Pioneer Jews: A New Light in the Far West.* NY: First Mariner Books, 2000.

Rosenbaum, Fred. *Visions of Reform: Congregation Emanu-el and the Jews of San Francisco,* Berkeley: Judah L. Magnes Museum, 2000.

Stevenson, Robert Louis. *Travels With a Donkey; An Internal Voyage; The Silverado Squatters,* ed. by Trevor Royle. Rutland, VT: J.M. Dent, 1993.

Sullivan, Charles. *Napa Wine: A History.* SF: Wine Appreciation Guild, 1994.

Weinstein, Miriam. *Yiddish: A Nation of Words.* S. Royalton, NJ: Steerforth Press, 2001.

Wolin, Penny. *The Jews of Wyoming: Fringe of the Diaspora.* Cheyenne, WY: Crazy Woman Creek Press, 2000.

Zwerdling, Alex. *Improvised Europeans.* NY: Basic Boooks, 1998.

—"The Story of Napa Leather," unpublished manuscript. Napa: Sawyer Tannery, 1944 and 1946.

Dorfman , Elaine and Caroline Crawford, interviewers. "Alfred Fromm: Wines, Music and Lifelong Education," 1986, 87. Berkeley, CA: Community Oral History Project, Bancroft Library.

Hicke, Carole, interviewer. "Albert Brounstein, Diamond Creek Vineyards: The Significance of Terroir in the Vineyard." Berkeley: The Regents of the University of California, 1998.

Hicke, Carole, interviewer. "Diamond Creek Vineyards: The Significance of

Terroir in the Vineyard," Berkeley: The Regents of the University of
California, 2000.
Rainer, Joseph T. "A Revolution in Trust? Character, Class, and Sectionalism
and the Paradoxes of Mercantile Confidence." *http://www2.h-net.msu.edu*
Rockaway, Robert. "Zionism: The National Liberation Movement of the
Jewish People," at *www.azm.org/essays/rockaway/.html*
Rosenblum, Jonathan. "Get Me to the Church on Time." *Jerusalem Post*
International Edition, 1-5-2001.
Spiro, Rabbi Ken . "Crash Course in Jewish History." *www.aish.com*
Teiser, Ruth. "Alfred Fromm: Marketing Wine and Brandy," Berkeley: The
Regents of the University of California, Berkeley, 1984.

Calistoga Tribune
Jewish Bulletin of Northern California
Napa County Reporter
Napa Daily Journal
Napa Register
Napa Sentinel
Napa Weekly Register
Pacific Echo
St. Helena Star
San Francisco Call
San Francisco Chronicle

Index

A

Abramowicz family: Harvey (Chaim) 114, 115; Luba 114; Myrna
	115, 149, 150
AIPAC: 165
Alaska Commercial Company: 45, 46
Alberti, Karl: 67
Alden (merchant): 27, 37, 168
Alden and Levinson: 169
Alfred Greenbaum & Co.: 59
Algeria: Algiers 104, 105; Oran 104
Altamura, George: 82
Angele's Restaurant: 153
anti-Semitism 3, 7, 25, 55, 59, 69, 80, 85, 92, 93, 95, 109, 126,
	144, 160, 162, 166
Arabs: 69, 103
Arbeiter Rings: 66
Ashkenazi Jews: 6, 13, 29, 164
Auberge du Soleil: 153
Australia: 55
Austria: 13, 65, 83, 155

B

B'nai B'rith: 79, 102, 109, 173
Baginsky, Yvonne: 172
Bale, E.T.: 15
Balfour Declaration: 68
Balzer, H.: 32
Bamburg, W.: 65
Bank of America: 124
Bank of Napa: 21, 40
Barnett, E.: 14

Battat, Marcia: 165
Baum, Rudolph: 168
Baylinson, Ben: 96, 121
Beaulieu Viineyard: 155
Begelspecker, Max: 20
Belgium: 92
Bell, Theodore: 42, 71, 72, 73
Beringer, Jacob: 50
Bernstein family: 127, 128, 138
Biber family: 57
Bickoff family: Ellie 76, 96, 97; Gussie 76; Mel 76, 96, 97; Sam 76, 96
Biehle Sisters: See Biber
Bien family: Karola 93, 94, 173; Richard 173
Birnbaum, Jan: 154
Bistro Don Giovanni: 153
Bistro Jeanty: 153
Bloch, M.: 27, 168
Block famiily: Alvin Lee 121, 122, 163, 165; Kevin 163
Bloom, Carolyn: 165
Boitano, Jim: 143
Bonaparte, Napoleon: 12, 13, 55, 134
Boston: 10, 68, 141
Boukofsky, Gustave: 19, 20
Boxer, Barbara: 149
Brandeis, Loius: 68
Brandt, James: 161
Brannan, Sam: 16, 31, 32, 33, 35, 45
Brazil: Recife 9, 10, 94
Brewster's: 116
Bronfman family: Edgar 155; Ekiel and Mindel 54; Sam 54, 72, 74, 91, 106, 126, 128; Samuel II 155
Broude, Rabbi Samuel: 173
Brounstein family: Al 73, 128-133, 138-139; Harry 73

Broverman, Don and Dan: 83
Brun & Chaix: 60

C
Cahen,Soloman: 20
California Wine Association (CWA): 59, 60, 61, 62
California Wine Institute: 106
Calistoga: 15, 31- 35, 43, 60, 64-65, 124, 130, 132, 139, 154
Canada 39, 72, 74
Casper, Abe: 83
Castner, William: 50
Catahoula Restaurant: 154
Catahoula Parish: 54, 154
Catholicism: 11, 61, 71, 85, 99, 106, 110, 112, 136, 172
CBS:108, 109, 113, 114, 118-122, 124, 142, 143, 147, 160, 162, 174 (see also Congregation Beth Sholom)
Chameleon Winery: 160
Charles Krug Winery: 138
Charleston, SC: 10, 115
Charlup family: 96, 100
Chicago: 53, 54
Chiles, Joe: 14
China: 16, 26, 44, 56
Christian Brothers Winery: 91, 126, 157-158
CIA Greystone: 157- 158 (see also Greystone)
City of Paris department store: 41, 106
Civil War: 19, 24, 26, 43-45, 49
Clinton, Bill: 149
Clos Pegase Winery:139, 160
Cohen family: Alice Muscatine 110; Orville 110
Cohen, H.: 32
Cohen, M:. 20

Cohn, Rabbi Elkan: 168
Columbus, Christopher: 8, 9
Communism: 53, 55, 65-66, 68, 78
Congregation Beth Sholom 108, 111, 116, 145, 148, 159, 161, 165 (see also CBS)
Congregation Emanu-el: 161, 165
Conservative Judaism:112, 113, 114, 159, 163
Cook's Imperial Champagne: 105-106
Corlett, Robert: 41
Cortes, Hernando: 9
Count Freyenstine 47
Cranston, Alan: 149
Czars: 7, 55, 66; Alexander II 52; Alexander III 52; Nicholas II 56, 66
Czechoslovakia: 78, 88, 90

D
Dachau: 90
Darvi, Bella: 105
Daume, John: 138
de Hirsch, Baron: 53, 54, 55, 82, 154; Clara Bischoffsheim, 53, 54
de Torres, Luis: : 8, 9
Dean & Deluca: 156, 159
DeDomenico, Mildred and Vincent: 122
Democratic Party: 64, 71, 72, 80, 123, 149
Denmark: 88
Depression, Great: 77, 79, 80, 93
Diageo: 155
Diamond Creek Winery: 130, 133, 160
Dinkelspiel, H.G.W. and Moses: 68
Domaine Chandon Winery:132
Dreyfus, Benjamin: 59

E

Eisenstark, Howard: 174
Ellis Island: 40, 53, 54, 114, 125, 150
England: 5, 13, 68, 69, 87, 89, 91, 92, 108, 134
Estee, Morris 59
Euster's 116

F

Faulkenstein, J.N.: 168
Finkelstein, Sam: 78
Finkelstein family: Art 54, 137, 138, 162; Bunnie Matz 137, 138;
      Judd 137
Ford, Henry: 80
Fountaingrove Winery: 105
France: 5, 9, 24, 26, 85, 90, 92, 104, 105, 131, 134, 140
Freed, David: 159, 160, 161
French Laundry: 153
Friedberg, Morris: 33, 34, 35
Friedman, Larry and Rachel: 116
Friedman, Herman: 54
Fromm family: Alfred 91, 106; Hanna 126; Max 91
Fromm & Sichel: 91
Fromm Institute for Lifelong Learning 126
fur traders: 3, 44, 45
furniture merchants: 11, 18, 21, 46, 58, 59, 75, 76, 96, 101, 116

G

Galewsky family: D. 28; Emanuel 28, 72, 73; Joe 28, 72, 74, 122;
      Rebecca 20, 28, 73; Sarah 28; Simon 20
Galicia: 65
Galveston Plan: 54, 55
Gau, William: 50

Geisenheim University: 90, 91

Gelvani Winery:160

Gemstone Winery:160

Germany: 5, 12, 13, 16, 32, 48, 63, 69, 85-91, 95, 107, 108, 114, 124, 145, 165; Barntrup 85, 86, 165; Bavaria 19, 48, 90, 100, 114, 167; Berlin 86, 89; Cologne 89; Frankfurt 5, 43, 87; Fuerth 87, 88; Hamburg 32, 86; Mainz 88, 90; Oldenburg 89

Gerstle, Lewis: 45

Gesford, Henry: 68

Getleson, Henry: 32-35

Gold Rush: 15- 18, 21, 24, 25, 30, 31, 32, 38, 39, 40, 57, 74, 113, 169

Goldberg, Mrs. C.: 43

Goldberg, Stella: 43

Golds, John: 41

Goldsmith, Julius: 20

Goldstein, Bunny: 175

Goldstein, Emanuel: 59

Goldstein, Rabbi Morris: 171

Gomberg, Lou: 106

Goodman family: Abraham 29, 72, 74,123, 124, 168; Jake 72, 123; Julius 72, 123; Katie 123

Goodman, James and George: 168-169

Gordon, "Chick": 83, 119

Gordon, Sam: 74, 75, 82, 171

Grauss, Felix: 35, 64, 65

Great Britain 68, 69, 92

Greystone: 60 (see also CIA Greystone)

grocery merchants: 11, 19

Grossman, Harry and Sam: 99

Guggenheim family: 5

guild system: 4, 12, 13

H

H. Sichel & Sohne: 91
Haas family: 5, 18, 19, 28, 40, 44; David 18, 21, 27, 35; Martin
    18, 21; Solomon 18, 21
Haas, Samuel: 18
Haber, Ferdinand: 59, 61
Hadassah: 115, 118
Hagafen Winery: 155, 160
Haller,M.: 18, 21
hardware merchants:11, 19, 40, 41, 42, 115
Harmon, Robert: 153
Hatt Building: 153
Hebrew Aid Society: 52, 79
Hedgeside Winery: 59
Heine family: Donna 119, 120, 161; Ernie 119, 120; Nancy 119,
    120
Hellman, Isaias: 59
Hennessey, Dr. E.Z.: 38
Herzl, Theodore: 68
Heymann, Ed: 50
High Holy Days: 38, 96, 107, 119
Hillcrest Winery: 60
Hitler, Adolph: 85, 87, 90, 92, 93
Holland: 9, 88, 92, 125
Holocaust: 102, 116, 118, 131, 141, 145, 146
Howland, Emma: 21

I

ILGWU: 66-67
Inglenook Winery: 59
Isaacs, C.: 19
Israel: 8, 34, 36, 103, 104, 112, 119, 131, 132, 141, 148, 155,
    165, 174; Binyamini 165; Jerusalem 2, 138; Tel Aviv 100;

Zichron Yaakov 165
Israelsky family: 20, 96
IWW: 67, 68

J
J&H Schwartz 41
Jacobson, M.: 33
Japan: 56, 98, 99, 111, 139
Jasnau, Max: 67
jewelry trade: 3, 11, 20, 96, 97, 98, 102, 109
Jewish Community of the Napa Valley: 122, 165
Jewish Defense League (JDL): 144, 145, 146, 147
Johnson, Andy: 124
Johnson, Bert and Rozaline: 101
Judd's Hill Winery:138, 160

K
Kahn, Howard and Zoe: 165
Katz family: Bruno 88; Egon 85, 86, 87, 88, 93, 165
Katz family: Reuben 67, 158; Reuven 67
Kaufman family: Al and Doris 56-59, 75-76, 96, 100, 101 (see also Biber); Rozaline 58, 75, 96, 100, 101
Kelly, Austin: 131
Kessler, Corby: 174
Kester, J.H.: 20
KKK: 71, 74, 75, 143, 147-148
Kopstein, Rabbi David: 113, 173
Koret of California: 135
Kornell, Hanns: 90, 91, 105-106, 124, 126, 128, 136
Korns, A.: 168
Kosch, Arnold: 64
kosher: 78, 95, 106, 112, 140, 155
Kristallnacht: 86, 87, 89, 90, 95

Kronberg family: 36, 39
Krug, Charles: 50
Kufflevitch, Al: 56, 75, 96 (see also Kaufman)

L
Lachman, Henry: 60
Lachman & Jacobi: 61
Lakeport: 27, 35
Laube, Jim: 128
Lauter family: 29, 169
Lazarus, Emma: 24, 53, 69
Lazarus, Joe: 96, 113, 119, 121
Lazarus family: Julia Straus 26; Leland 123; Leopold 24-
     27, 30, 46, 50, 123; Sylvain 30, 123
Lazarus & Levy: 27
Lazarus & Straus: 33
Lebner, J.C.: 64
Lerman, Golden: 145
Lenson, Richard: 174
Level brothers: 24, 26-28
Levels, Guillaume: 168
Levene, Mr. and Mrs.: 43
Levin, Philip: 78
Levinson & Strauss: 37
Levinson family: 16, 72, 74, 168; Annie 36, 39, 43; Charlie 37,
     38, 39, 42, 97; Clara 39; Freedman 16, 17, 21, 36; Joe 38,
     39; Sarah 37, 39
Levinson's Pharmacy: 38, 39
Levison family: Helen, Hyman, Minnie 43
Levy, Abe: 37
Levy, Daniel: 168
Levy, E.J. and M.S.: 169
Levy family: Barnard 39, 96; Claire 97; Harold 98

Levy, Janett: 26, 168
Lieberstein, Gary: 147, 151, 165
Lightner, Joel: 32
Lindbergh, Charles 80
Linn family: 117-118
Lonsdale, Howard: 143, 146
LRICo: 156
Lutge, August: 65

M
Manasse family: 65, 96; Amelia Hellwig 43; Ed 44; Emanuel 43-45; Henry J. 44
Margolis, Boyd: 83
Marshall, Helene Glickfeld: 165
Martin, Harry: 146, 147, 163
Marx, John: 95, 96, 119
mashgiach: 78
Masons: 33, 122, 173; Royal Arch 61
Mautner family: David 147; Elizabeth Ellis 141, 142, 145, 146; Jerry 141, 142, 143, 144, 145, 146, 147, 148; John 142, 143, 146; Michael 141
May Laws: 52
McEachran, C.T.: 50
McPherson, Harry: 108
Memphis: 29, 125, 169
Mendelsohn family: David 148, 165; Donna 103, 174
Mendelssohn, Felix and Moses: 12
merchants 2, 3, 4, 5, 17, 20, 21, 23, 27, 28, 29, 30, 56, 59, 61, 71, 111, 115, 124, 153, 165
Mervyn's Department Store: 173
Messianic Judaism:113
Metz, Ferdinand: 158
Metzger, Tom: 143, 146

Mexican-American War: 14, 16, 40

Mexico: 9, 15, 25, 26, 70, 71, 74, 83, 84, 101, 102, 123, 132

Meyer, Lulu: 43

Meyer family: Benton 59; Ellie 76, 98 (see also Bickoff); Isadore 58, 97; Lena 97; Wesley 59, 96, 97, 98, 99, 102, 109

Meyers Jewelers: 59, 97, 102, 109

Meyers, George: 46

Michalski family: Fela (Felicia) 92, 100, 114; Henry 100, 118, 131; Joseph 92, 100, 114

Miller, John F.: 45

Mondavi family: Robert 134, 135; Tim 135

Monticello: 20

Morgan, Jeff: 159

Morganthau, Henry: 93

Morris, Mervyn: 173

Mount Veeder Winery: 128

Mouton-Rothschild: 131, 134, 135

Mt. View Hotel: 154

Muscatine (Mushkatin) family: Alice (see Cohen) 110; Bertha Greenberg 111; Charles, 173; Sam 110, 112

Muslims: 8, 69, 112, 165

N

N. Fromm, Wine Growers and Shippers 91

Napa, city of: 15, 17, 18, 19, 20, 21, 24, 25, 27, 28, 35, 36, 37, 38, 39, 40, 41, 42, 43, 44, 46, 60, 65, 67, 72, 75, 81, 82, 83, 93, 95, 96, 97, 98, 99, 102, 103, 104, 106, 107, 108, 109, 110, 111, 112, 115, 116, 117, 118, 119, 121, 122, 131, 142, 143, 145, 146, 147, 148, 149, 150, 153, 154, 156, 159, 161, 163

Napa Valley Coffee Roasting Company: 162

Napa Valley (Community) College: 108, 148, 149

Napa Valley Emporium: 147

Napa Valley Vintners' Association: 128

Nazis: 85- 90, 92, 93, 104, 144, 145, 165, 172
Nemko family: Barbara (Podridsky) Padrid, 149, 150, 165; Marty
    150
Nevada City: 18
New Orleans: 24, 26, 29, 60
New York: 10, 14, 16, 19, 20, 32, 41, 43, 49, 53, 55, 57, 58, 59,
    61, 69, 84, 91, 94, 104, 107, 110, 111, 114, 138, 141, 142,
    150, 153, 154, 156, 165
Newport: 10, 25, 29
Niebaum, Gustav: 45, 46, 59, 133
Niebaum-Coppola Winery: 46
Norris, Debbie: 144
North Dakota: 54
Nuremberg Laws: 86
Nussbaum family: Annie 115; Harris 116; Minnie, 116; Morris
    115, 116; Rachel 116

O

Oakville: 46, 60, 100, 156
Ochs family: 5
Odd Fellows: 18, 20, 26, 42, 168
On the Vine: 162
Oppenheim family: 5
Orthodox Judaism: 33, 55, 68, 78, 87, 96, 107, 108, 111-114, 125,
    126, 147, 163, 164
Ostjuden: 13, 33, 34, 68

P

Pacific Echo: 19
Pacific Union College: 121
Pale of Settlement: 7, 13, 52
Palestine: 3, 68, 69, 92, 100, 103
paper merchants: 3, 11, 18

Pastcan, Richard: 174
Paul Masson Winery: 106
peddlers: 11, 16, 20, 28, 29, 58, 70, 76, 81, 83, 84, 110, 116
Pennsylvania: 10
Percelay family: Anne 118, 119; Eliot 118, 174
Peres, J.J.: 125
Perl, P.E.: 20
Perlman family: Mike 147, Sandi Rubin 147, 148 (see also
      Rubin)
Philadelphia: 10
Piatti restaurant: 153
Pittsburgh: 67, 158
Placerville, Indiana: 32
pogroms: 7, 52, 56, 170
Poland: 6, 7, 65, 76, 92, 115, 125, 150, 172; Cracow 94; Warsaw
      56, 94
Pope Valley 14, 20, 40, 71, 75, 76, 96, 100, 139
Port Arthur: 56
Portugal: 5, 9, 125
Posert, Harvey: 80, 125, 165, 174
Posner, Larry: 174
postmasters: 21, 27, 64, 72, 122
Press, Ada: 162
Prohibition: 62, 63, 71, 74, 77, 78, 91, 128, 132, 155
Protestants: 11, 62, 71, 80, 112, 163
Prussia: 13, 16, 19, 43

Q
quicksilver mining:40, 67, 171

R
Rabbis: 4, 57, 73, 78, 88, 89, 108, 111, 113, 120, 121, 122, 131,
      141, 145, 160, 161

Raboy, Asher: 165
Ravensrueck: 88, 134
Reconstructionist Judaism: 113
Reform Judaism:12, 13, 33, 34, 36, 38, 55, 68, 113, 125, 141,
    159, 161, 163
Relationship Resources Unlimited: 160
Renewal Judaism:113
Republican Party: 123
Revolutionary War: 10
Rhode Island: 10, 29
Richard Mendelson Winery: 160
Ridge Vineyards: 130
Robert Mondavi Winery: 127
Rock Island, Illinois: 54, 103
Romans: 2, 3, 12
Romania: 52, 69, 70, 83
Romanovs (see czars)
Roosevelt, Franklin: 80, 92, 93
Rosenbaum family: 46, 49, 59; August 46; Bertie 46, 47, 48;
    Fritz 46
Rosenbaum, Simon: 46
Rosenberg family: George 107, 108, 111, 112, 114, 118, 119,
    159; Lottie 107 (see also Rosenthal)
Rosenberger family: 69, 71 Sara 101, 123, 124; Zoltan 70, 84, 85,
    101, 123, 124
Rosenthal, Elizabeth: 87, 88, 93
Rosenthal family: Bella 95, 96, 106, 108, 112; Fred 95, 106;
    Lottie 95, 106, 107
Rother, E.: 32
Rothman, Nat: 81, 82, 83; Harry 83
Rothschild family: 5, 6; Baron Philippe 134, 135; Lilli 134;
    Philippine 134, 135
Rouas familly: Albert 153; Alexandrine Venezia 173; Ardath 152;
    Armand 104; Bettina 152, 153; Claude 104, 152, 153;

Claudia 152, 153
Rough Rider: 81-83, 96, 102, 109, 111, 119, 121, 124, 142, 148
Rubin, Irv: 145, 147 (see also Perlman)
Rudd Center for Professional Wine Studies: 157, 158
Rudd family: Leslie 155, 156, 158, 159, 161; Sam 155
Rudd Foundation: 157
Rudd Institute: 157
Rudd Vineyards & Winery: 156
Russia: 7, 33, 45, 52, 54- 56, 59, 65, 66, 70, 76, 92, 100, 110,
        114, 135; St. Petersburg 56
Rutherford: 78, 132
Ryan, Tim: 158

S
Salmina Winery: 124
Salomon, Haym: 10
Salomonson, Julius: 18, 20
Salvador, Francis: 10
San Francisco 15- 19, 23, 25- 27, 29, 32, 33, 36, 39, 40, 41, 43,
        44- 46, 47, 56- 60, 68, 72-75, 81, 83, 93, 95, 96, 105-107,
        114- 116, 122, 123, 126, 136, 152- 154, 159, 168, 169
Sange family: Alexander 135; Benjamin 136; Irene Weinberg 136;
        Leon 135, 136, 162; Nancy Noll 136, 140
Saskatchewan: 54
Sawyer, F.A,: 44
Sawyer Tannery: 44, 79, 156
Schiff, Jacob: 53, 54
Schoenberger Kabinett: 90
Schorr, Abraham: 78
Schwab family: 5
Schwartz family: 40; Adelheide Vogel 41; David 42, 43; Florella
        43; Henry 41; Jake 40; Joseph 41- 43; Mathilda Weil 41;
        Max 42; Muriel 43

Schwartz, Isaac: 43
Schwarz family: David 40, 43, 71; Emma 43; Herman 40, 43;
    Lizzie Fleishman 40; Max 40, 43: Will 40, 43, 65
Schwarz Block: 42
Schwarz Hardware: 41, 169, 170
Seagram's Distillers: 72, 74, 155
Secular Humanistic Judaism: 114, 125
Sephardic Jews: 8, 9, 10, 11, 24, 26, 28, 29, 53, 94, 104, 105, 125,
    164, 168
Serlis, Harry: 125
Shasta City: 32
Shearith Israel: 10
Sherith Israel: 123, 171
Shrem, Jan and Mitsuuko:138, 139
Sichel family: 5: Franz 91, 106, 126
Siebreight, P.: 64
Silver, Diane: 173
Silverado Country Club: 59
Simon, Sara: 83, 84
Six Day War :131, 132
Skalli, Michael: 140
Slensburg prison: 88
Sloss, Louis: 45
Snowden, Scott: 146
Soloman, Jerome: 173
South Africa: 55, 67
South America: 16, 54, 55
Spain: 8, 9, 125
Spanish Inquisition: 9
Squirrel Hill: 67, 158
Spittler, Bob: 144
St. Helena 20, 24-30, 33, 35, 37, 40, 44, 48, 50, 67, 71, 72, 78,
    80, 90, 122-125, 132, 136, 138, 152, 156, 157, 162
St. Supery Winery: 140, 160

Stalin, Joseph: 100
Steckter, Jack: 79, 99
Steen family: Alan 54, 137, 138; Charlene 137, 138, 148, 150;
  Eva 138; Larry 138; Sarah 138
Sterling Vineyards: 155
Stevenson, Robert Louis: 34, 35
Stoer, Leo: 174
Straus family: E. A. 26; Janett 26, 27; Joe 26, 27
Strauss, Abe: 37
Sunday Fun Day: 116, 144
Sutro, C:. 32
Swartz, Peter: 40
Synagogue in the Vineyard: 159, 160

T
Tallman, D.S.: 21
Tannenbaum family: (see Abramowicz); Joshua 114,
115
Temple Emanu-el 36, 39, 43, 45, 68
Theresienstadt: 88, 90
Thomann, John: 50
tobacco dealers: 9, 18, 21, 27, 39
Treblinka: 88
Trepp family: Leo 88, 89, 108, 111, 120, 121, 131, 145; Miriam
  89
Tschelistcheff, Andre: 130, 139
Tulare County: 25
Turn Vereins: 42
Turton, Luther: 41

U
UCC Vineyards: 160
Uncle Sam Winery: 60

United Workmen: 168
Unity Hose Company: 37, 38, 39

V

Vallejo: 15, 18, 25, 58, 59, 75, 82, 96, 97, 101, 106, 108, 143
Vernier, Paul: 106
Vida, Rabbi George: 173
Vietnam: 131
Visigoths: 8, 9
Vogel, Julius: 43

W

Washington, George: 10
Wasserman, A: 45
Weidler, Julian: 83, 102, 104, 109, 111, 148, 165
Weil famiily: 170 (see also Schwartz)
Weinberger family: 48, 59; Hannah Rabbe 49, 51; John C. 48, 49,
        50; Minnie 49
Weinberger Winery: 49
Weinlander, August: 19
Weinstein, Dan: 83, 111
Weinstock, Sam: 83
Weir family: 132; Ernie 154, 165; Irit 155, 165; Jonathan 155;
        Maya 155; Tamar 155
Wells, Fargo Express Company: 21, 27
White, Rabbi David: 160, 161, 173
White Aryan Resistance: 143-146
White Papers: 69
White Sulphur Springs: 23, 31
Whitehall Lane Winery: 138, 148
wine: 3, 6, 30, 31, 46, 48-51, 54, 59-63, 72, 73, 76, 77, 90, 91, 95,
        105, 106, 122, 124-130, 132- 139, 148, 150, 153- 160,
        165, 166

Winehaven: 60, 63
WineSpirit: 160
Winkler, B.F.: 20
Wolfenbittel: 90
World War I: 62, 63, 65, 66, 68, 69, 71, 74, 111, 134
World War II: 98, 134, 100, 166, 171

X
Xenophobia 11, 62, 71, 126, 118, 166

Y
Yiddish: 6, 85, 107, 115
York, Constable: 118
York, E.M.: 50
Yount, George: 15
Yountville: 78, 154
Yudnich, Joseph: 71, 76

Z
Zapolski + Rudd 156
Zellerbach,William: 169
Zion: 10, 68, 69, 80, 100, 103, 104, 155
Zubrick & Keifer 18

Ellie Meyer's
Kosher Dill Pickles*

Wash cucumbers thoroughly.

Cover cucumbers in water and soak for 24 hours in refrigerator.

Wash, drain, and pack tightly in quart jars. To each jar add:

> 1 tsp. pickling spice
>
> 2-3 bay leaves
>
> 1-2 cloves garlic
>
> 1 small red serrano or other hot pepper
>
> fresh dill, with stem
>
> 1 tbsp. white vinegar

In a separate bowl prepare:

> water to fill jars, with 1/4 cup kosher salt for each quart of water

Pour brine over cucumbers and fill to top. Over each filled jar place:

> 2 grape leaves (washed)

Screw on tops loosely. Ferment at room temperature until liquid in the jars becomes cloudy (about 5-7 days). If brine level drops, replenish. When fermentation is complete, sterilize canning lids and tighten onto jars. Refrigerate. Enjoy.

                    SHELF LIFE IS VERY SHORT !

*adapted from "Fun with Food," by Pam Hunter, *Napa Register*, 10-22-1974